SHINE IN YOUR LANE

BELIEVE YOU CAN SHINE AND YOU WILL

COACH KURINN WRIGHT

This book is designed to help you think, live, and love better by knowing who you are, what's inside you, and how to apply your best self to life.

COACH WRIGHT CONSULTING

KWRIGHTCOACHING.COM

"The Moon cannot be a Star nor can a Star be the Moon, yet they both shine." – Coach Kurinn Wright

DEDICATION

I dedicate this book to my mother, Janice Wright; my aunt, Althea Raines; my favorite person on Earth, D'unTre Raines; my sisters, Shalon and Rhonesha Wright; and my fathers, Jeffrey Brooks and Lester Michael Wright. If these people were not in my life, among others, I don't know who or where I would be. They have all played vital roles in my journey of becoming the woman I am today.

ACKNOWLEDGMENTS

I want to acknowledge Nkansa Landis Casterlow for consistently encouraging me to write this book. I also want to acknowledge my extended family, the women who've played a role in my journey in one way or another: Ni'ger Brisbane, Kwajelyn Jackson, Nicole K. Jones, Dr. Rhonda Davis Anderson, Venesha Scott, Valarie Tutuh, Deidra Dezell, Tiffany Glass, Skip McDonald, and a friend I could never have found had I not been open to where my path would lead me, Margarita Jerden.

Last but not least, I now acknowledge Roderick C. Ford. He helped me to see myself from a perspective where I could dig deeper into the meaning of everything around me and fully understand life through the eyes of others and why it really matters. Through him I learned more about myself than I anticipated. I saw integrity, commitment, responsibility, giving, and so much more became illuminated in my character simply by connecting with a like mind—all while allowing God to increase as I decreased. Those who know me know a genuine person who puts on no face other than a real representation of a discovered self. An ever evolving, unafraid woman aiming to live right and love God through all of her faults and flaws. A woman who is *simply who she is* while desiring to help others come into their own as who they were created to be.

To God, and every person I have encountered at any point in my life... with you I am everything, and without you I am nothing.

CONTENTS

Table of Contents

INTRODUCTION

"Energy is far more than strength, electricity, or drive; it is also the radiating connection we have between ourselves and surrounding people, places, and things."

– *#coachwright*

What does it mean to shine? It means not being led by what others have or what they're doing, but focusing on yourself. It means being intentional about discovering what you have and actively using it to attain everything you want. To shine in your lane means to not look around for what's already inside you. Every desire you have in business or personal life can be fulfilled by tapping into your core. Don't worry about what you see in others, wishing you could be like them or have their results. Once you realize you've been given something specific, you will see how limiting it is to compare or compete with anyone. We can't really be ourselves until we see ourselves. Take the sun for example. The sun holds a tremendous amount of energy. Most of the times, we can't bear to look directly at it for too long without our eyes being affected by its light; however, we can look at its circumference with ease. Imagine countless numbers of catalytic light circles or bubbles around the sun, near and far. Inside each bubble is a different degree of light. Your light represents your lane, where you pursue your greatness and live out your own destiny without comparing yourself to anyone. It is important that everyone finds his or her own path to shine and not infringe on another's. Otherwise, we miss our own opportunities to fully develop.

Once we begin to know ourselves better, we will more than likely understand that competing with others is a distraction meant to slow us down or throw us off course. Like the sun, your light will always shine when it needs to. In other words, the sun does not force itself out during the night to compete with the moon because that is not its natural order; the night is not the sun's lane. In the same way, your light will naturally appear and the right people and things will be attracted to you when you intently focus on *your* purpose. Try not to be concerned with the distance between someone else's light and the sun versus yours. The shine you see in others is not meant to draw you into their lane. It is simply an invitation to exchange energy in an effort to fulfill each other in some way. With this in mind, keep your feet firmly planted.

In my lane, I wear several hats. When I became a certified life coach, I chose to specialize in life, business, and author coaching, as well as youth development. Life coaching just made sense with my background. I had spent over thirteen years in higher education, but the last four to five years had the biggest impact on my life. I worked as an advisor for non-traditional, at-risk college students. My role was to create action plans for their success, plans designed specifically for individual students with the goal to help them meet the requirements of remaining in school. I met with them frequently to track their progress toward graduation as they dealt with issues outside of the classroom that led them to my office in the first place. I learned that the issues most of them had were not related to the classroom as much as they were life issues. That forced me to figure out how to create life plans alongside their academic plans. My demographics were males and females between the ages of 18-65. I had been life coaching for years prior to getting a certification. What is a life coach if not someone who listens to others and helps them develop a plan to achieve better results?

***

Trust the process, allowing your instincts to be your guide. I remember having a two-year conversation with God before I was laid off from a university where I worked for nearly ten years. I told Him and everyone around me that I would be an entrepreneur, that this was my last job. I had no idea what I would be doing at the time, but I knew that I was a born leader who preferred to work alone or at least run my own business.

In my free time, I created hand-made art pieces as a stress-reliever to keep myself balanced. The entrepreneur in me became restless over time, so I decided to put on an art show. I selected the date of June 15th 2013. On June 1st I was called into the president's office and told that June 30th would be my last day. We must be ready for the next thing when we feel the energy of that thing approaching. The art show was beautifully done at a downtown loft. I sold many pieces and made the equivalent of one paycheck in three hours. I saw my ability to use *my* gifts up close, and the talents of the people around me to gain success. In hindsight, I can see how this was confirmation that I had what it took to be a successful entrepreneur. After the show, people came to me for advice on how to start a business, how to manage social media, how to appeal to particular audiences, and so on. I found myself driving to their homes and sitting in coffee shops to help them develop plans. As a result of this, I co-founded iNSPIRE Entrepreneurs, which was initially a giveback to a product line my business partner and I were working on together. The name was inspired by a message I heard where everything was driven by the letter (i). The message was giving insight on how we are in control of what we give to

12

the world. I was literally someone inspiring those who wanted to become entrepreneurs. Looking back, all of the pieces fell into place, and they always will when you connect your passion with your talents. Entrepreneurship is hard, but what makes it work or fail is the entrepreneur—his or her knowledge, passion, or lack thereof, and tenacity. Business coaching sought me out, and is now a natural part of my life with iNSPIRE Entrepreneurs.

***

I wrote my first poem at age nine, I began to write music at the age of fourteen, poetry consistently at eighteen, and short stories in my twenties. Now I write novels and non-fiction. I have published less than 10% of what I've written, but I realize that I had to mature into the type of writer I am meant to be. I still write and use pen names for some of my works, but the joy I get out of helping people achieve their goal of becoming published authors is almost unreal. As a writer and author coach, I have experience with not only assisting people with the writing process, but also publishing. I've self-published and launched publishing companies, which is a great skill for any author to possess. These are what I consider to be natural gifts. They are all connected, and I am fully aware that I am in my lane.

This particular book has a purpose beyond my wanting to help people see themselves into their own greatness. I too struggle in certain areas. These are the areas in which I am learning to handle differently, but doing so is a daily process. After working through the steps in this book, I now know what I have to strive for to become more like the version of myself I enjoy the most.

I want people all over the world to have access to every fiber of what I believe will make a great and positive impact in anyone who has the courage to S.H.I.N.E. If there is at least one thing that speaks to you, then I have done everything I was created to do in your life.

Whether you want to strengthen something you're passionate about or strengthen your weaknesses, this is an excellent tool for group and corporate coaching, motivating, staff retention, building healthier relationships (both business and personal), educating youth and adults on how to soar within their own positive attributes, and reaching one's maximum potential. When asked a question, please take the time to reflect on what is being asked, and feel free to journal your thoughts, emotions, and views as you move through this book.

S.H.I.N.E.I.N.Y.O.U.R.L.A.N.E.

CHAPTER 1

See Yourself

Chapter one is filled with self-reflection exercises designed to help you reach a healthy conclusion. These exercises may seem overwhelming to the average person, but you're not average, so pull out your journal, relax and let's get started.

Don't look left. Don't look right. Look at you! It's time to peel back the layers and remove the mask. Time to get real. Are you willing to be wholly transparent with the one person you've spent your entire life with? It's time to take a hard look at the very core of what could make or break your happiness and success in this life. How unstoppable or illimitable do you know yourself to be? On the other hand, how often do you hold back, doubt, or rethink your positions?

When God reaffirmed Abraham, He told him He would expand his descendants beyond the number of stars and grains of sand (Genesis 22:17). Imagine the Father standing beside you with His arm around your shoulder, with the moon lighting the night sky. You're standing at the cusp of the seashore and God tells you, "I will bless you as far as you can see." Yes, you see the stars and the sand, and even miles upon miles of water. But what is it in that moment that you envision? Are you looking at what's in front of you? Have you accepted the vision He gave specifically to you? How do you see yourself?

I NEED EVERY SEED

There are many factors that affect the way we see ourselves—from our perceived statuses to how we maneuver in society. However, for many people, one factor that can either boost or cripple the way we feel about ourselves is our past. This could go as far back to include our childhood experiences.

Some of us come from homes with stable, healthy environments while some of us come from so-called "broken" homes. I consider myself as someone who experienced both worlds. I grew up with two fathers, one mother and two sisters, and I am the middle child. We've lived in houses, Section 8 homes, the projects, and apartments. I've had everything I wanted (as a spoiled child would) and nearly nothing (living in poverty). I've seen drugs and alcohol up close and personal. I've watched smoke from a man's crack pipe dance in front of me while hanging out with the wrong friends, witnessed behavior that can't be explained with words, and at times been whipped for no logical reason while being cursed at. Having to confront such things made me fearless. So much so that as I sat on the porch until nightfall at eight years old, waiting for my mother to come home from a binge needing me to take care of her, I played the role of mom very easily. By the time I was a pre-teen, I'd had a gun pulled on me, and I'd pulled a gun on someone—not with the intention to shoot or kill but merely to protect myself. As drugs and alcohol destroyed parts of my family, I daydreamed about what I thought life would be like if I could erase all the negative effects this substance brought into my home.

Despite all of the "brokenness," I can also say that I had access to firm and healthy foundations. I still had an amazing life growing up. The things I mentioned are only parts of my journey. My sisters and I have always been very close. We were allowed to do our own grocery shopping at the ages of ten, eleven, and thirteen. We'd write three separate menus for breakfast, lunch, and dinner and put them on the fridge. Believe it or not, my mother would cook all meals three times a day. We were involved in all kinds of activities, my mother was very active at our school, and she would sometimes substitute teach with absolutely no degree. There was also Mickey, our dad, and my biological father, Jeffrey, who raised me too—Jeffrey was never out of the picture. I used to be ashamed of having two dads until I realized how much love I was blessed to get from them both—two protectors, two great men, and two different examples of how to love myself from a man's perspective. I watched Mickey walk to work and leave us the car every day. He took care of us like we were his only job. And Jeffrey always sent me home with three of any item, never to neglect my sisters.

My perspective of life always was and still is that with God I can do anything. Although I had been cursed out, beaten, suffered though my parents' divorce, was displaced for a short while, and grew up faster than the kids around me, I *saw* far more than I actually went through. All of my needs were met, I was taught how to show and gain respect, how to manage money, work hard, give and receive love, use my common sense, value myself, and at a very young age was blessed with an amount of wisdom that still surpasses my understanding today. I was shown love, and from a giving standpoint, I learned how to love unconditionally. I always saw myself bigger than where I was and what I was surrounded by. I felt in my heart that I was supposed to be more and do more. When I was thirteen years old I told myself I would be everything God created me to be, one hundred percent Kurinn. I wanted to experience every ounce of who I was supposed to be on this earth, and help everyone around me to do the same. I knew I had a choice of who I'd become one day.

At some point we all have to take responsibility for what we are exposed to. It is up to us as individuals to choose what to read, what we watch on television, where we go, and so on. I cringe inside when I hear conversations in which people list their childhood limitations and go on to say how they are not supposed to be where they are. Through my eyes, a person who grew up on welfare, had multiple kids at a young age and limited education is exactly someone who should turn out to be an attorney, an A-list actress, a doctor, or an entrepreneur. Why not? The odds are only odds because of our mindsets. These things are meant to ensue a level of discomfort to push you into greater, not to hold you back. Have you ever had a job that you hated so much you'd call in from the parking lot because you just couldn't force yourself to walk inside? That level of discomfort is the only saving grace to get you to act on what your instincts are telling you to do. Your past experiences have a role in your future. The same way you feel when you walk away from that job is the way you will feel when you fearlessly walk into your destiny.

I am sharing all of this with you to illustrate that you are not defined by your past. Those events are simply pieces to the bigger picture of your life. Regardless of whether you had a rosy or rocky past, you can use it for your benefit—as motivation to choose where you want to go and who you want to be. So the question now is this: How can you use your past to accomplish the desires of your heart and shine?

YES YOU! BUT WHEN, WHERE, AND WHY?

Take a long moment to think about how you see yourself. Also think about where you see yourself if nothing stood in your way. Are you teaching classes to underprivileged children in the U.S. or overseas, sending a plane for your friends to have lunch with you in Dubai once a month? Do you live in a loft that sits on a mountaintop where you can see the city lights from your bedroom? Do you see yourself driving a Tesla to a corporate office where you work for an import/export company? Do you see yourself as an entrepreneur with two kids and a spouse who doesn't have to work because your success affords you a lifestyle of financial freedom? Are you someone who hasn't been able to move about or get out of bed for years? Do you see yourself walking into the kitchen to prepare a meal for your family and friends?

Vision is so much more important than reality! Reality can be a settled mentality by accepting where you are as where you will always be. Vision—and your action upon that vision—has the power to take you from where you are to where you want to be. Sure we can take a look at DNA, but I have friends who were adopted—some who have met their biological parents and some who haven't. I believe it's fair to say that the core of their mindsets and life's experiences were shaped by the people who raised them and not particularly by their biological parents. I have one friend who's said to me, "I am nothing like my biological mother." While it is true that there are some important factors that come from one's DNA, they don't apply here as much as the self-assessment does, which is why we're not focusing on DNA. It's not about knowing where you came from in that sense but more so about your own life's experiences and choices that shape you into the person you become over time. Our lanes in life have everything to do with our perspectives, our visions, and our willingness to act (how we see, what we see, and what we're willing to do about it). You are not where you are by happenstance, and as an ever-evolving being, you have the ability to choose who you will ultimately become. If you are stuck trying to figure out how you see yourself or where you want to be, simply ask yourself the following powerful questions in Exercise A. Answer them boldly and honestly, then reflect.

Exercise A:

- Who am I?
- Am I the type of person I am attracted to?
- What are my strengths and weaknesses?
- What do I value?
- What drives me?
- If I could choose one thing to do for the rest of your life, what would it be?
- What is something I think about constantly? Is it a limitation, problem or resentment; or is it my future, plans, or current situation?
- Am I fulfilled at night before going to bed, or do I often feel that there is more to be done to complete my day?
- What do I spend the most hours of the day doing? What do I want to do with the most hours of my day? What stands between your answers to these two questions?
- What are my pressure points (what easily causes me to stress)?
- Do I investigate the things I want to know more about?

ARE YOU WHO YOU THINK YOU ARE?

This is a very important question, as it is crucial that you know who you are. If you're not sure, start off by asking yourself these key questions: Are you someone who never spends time alone? Have you had genuine breaks between relationships, or do you move from one to the next to avoid being alone? It can be difficult for you to truly know who you are if you are always absorbing other people's energy around you. Time alone is crucial because it makes space for necessary internal pruning that prepares you for certain experiences. Getting to know yourself alongside someone else shapes you instead of defining you. Besides, who are you taking into relationships if not a person who is carrying baggage from one to the next? Even if you do spend that time alone, it's not being alone that will help you become fully you—fully restored, or more aware—it's what you do in that alone time that makes you whole. Maximize what takes place when you're alone. Don't push the pause button; actually live. Make mistakes and clean them up. Read and learn the fullness of what you're taking in. Try new things to see what you like. Do something you don't normally do like cooking, traveling outside of your home state, taking a class, or building a genuine relationship with someone of the opposite sex without expectations of romance. These suggestions (when acted out) have been helpful for many.

If you're still wondering if you are who you think you are, also ask yourself where and how you are spending your energy. The difference between the two will either amplify or dull your shine. At the end of the day, this radiating of energy all boils down to character—not just what you do but more importantly who you are. Whatever is on the inside will manifest on the outside.

Let me explain. Many of us are familiar with the saying "watch your mouth." We think we need to address our behaviors by what comes out of our mouths, but a changed mind will take care of that. What are our thoughts and motives? What factors promote the things that come out of us? Our eyes and ears are our most precious assets—more than our mouths. With even small amounts of time invested in looking at or listening to anything over a consistent period, we can align our behavior. Each of us are specifically designed for and with a purpose, so we must pay attention to where we fix our thoughts and what we entertain. One astounding fact about how we were created is that even if we've consumed so much of something that has diluted the best of us, we have the power to be restored. The good thing about restoration for humans is that it has no limit. Nothing separates us from the power of grace. All we have to do is want it.

CHARACTER MATTERS

Our actions, words, and image all contribute to our character. Our actions have everything to do with where we are right now. If we think about our role in other people's lives, shouldn't it be to leave them enhanced after having an encounter with us? Something as simple as communication maintains the power to destroy relationships if not used effectively. Knowing this, it should be easy to accept the fact that your actions and words should align. You have the right to change your mind, but when it involves someone else you must communicate that change as to not negatively affect an expectation *you*'ve set. The better we communicate, the more likely we are to save our relationships, protect our character, and live with integrity. Putting ourselves in the shoes of others helps to shift our thinking and is a great way to train ourselves into considering our actions before we act. Although *you* may know why you didn't keep your commitment, and you may have a valid reason, the other person is left to conclude his or her own idea about who you are over time. A lack of clear communication can cost you their respect, and if work-related, their business. Regardless of whether you're dealing with a stranger, a friend, or a family member, your interaction with one is just as important as it is with the other. Strangers should not get the best of you, everyone should. What could your current actions cost you? Tell yourself out loud what you have to lose by *not* keeping your word. Think about these things when making any commitments or decisions. Although none of us are blameless, and we *will* make many mistakes, the idea here is to do your best to live better, to draw nearer the positive energy for the things you desire in life by making thoughtful decisions.

Exercise B:

Create an outline. You can use your resume as a guide, or create a bulleted outline from scratch. Include your name, age, occupation, hobbies, etc. Describe your personality (outgoing, introverted, helpful, honest, and so on), and give a short description of who you are based on these things. Consider it a "life" biography. Write out your short-term goals, and in a separate area, your long-term goals. Be as detailed as possible so that when you read this aloud you will hear and receive all the great things you have to offer—and all of the great things to come.

Exercise C:

On a separate sheet of paper, write down the following and be open to the idea that there may be some things that please you and some that don't.

- What are you known for by others?
- What is the one thing you struggle with the most? (Running late, telling lies, snapping at people, being loud, etc.)?
- What have several people told you about yourself that isn't necessarily positive?
- Do you have issues within your circle of friends, co-workers, or family?
- Do most of the people around you seem to be annoying or annoyed by you?
- Does it appear that no matter what you do, things still aren't working in your favor?
- Do you have a clear conscience?
- Is there something you keep doing that you are not proud of?

THE STRENGTH IN TRANSPARENCY

Seeing yourself requires total transparency with yourself to overcome any undesirable character flaws. Just like my past and your past, exposing yourself prevents others from exposing you. We don't expose ourselves for the purpose of beating anyone to it; we do so in an effort to acknowledge where we once were versus where we are now. It's our testimony.

My transparency is a formidable strength, as there's no one in this world who can bring up my past or a family member's past and offend me. It needed it to be what it was for me to be who I am today. Once we acknowledge our pasts and flaws, we must take the hard steps to move beyond them. Whether you struggle with addiction, compulsion, cheating, stealing, etc., you can overcome. But the longer we hide behind the things that were not necessarily positive, the longer the power cord between our future and us maintains a shortage.

Have you ever plugged your cell phone into the wall only to have to hold the cord a certain way for it to charge, and every time you moved your hand it stopped charging? You find yourself having to over-accommodate for the situation when you could be doing something else while the phone takes care of itself. This is exactly what certain areas of our lives are like when we fail to simply buy a new cord (take care of the core issue within ourselves). Even as simple as a person who procrastinates within their own life by failing to prepare for events they know are coming, no one is asking them to change the way they operate, but when that way begins to negatively affect other people, then yes, we are asking that those behaviors change. Mediocrity is not everyone's cup of tea; therefore, it should not be forced on others just because it's how someone chooses to go about life. When we deal with others, it's okay to raise the standards of your actions to meet theirs, but you shouldn't have to lower your standards to meet anyone where they are. We all have a responsibility to each other, and it's not to drag others down a sinking rabbit hole. Maintain an even keel by keeping your standards in alignment with where you see yourself going and by helping to uplift those who are not yet there. We are all great once we use what's in us to shine in areas where others may need to see the light while trying to take their first or next step. *Our* lack of shine prevents someone around us from also shining.

VIEWS FROM THE OUTSIDE

The key to building positive relationships is all about *your* image in *someone else's* eyes. While set the tone, what others see in us is a representation of something we're putting out there, be it the way we dress, act, sound, or smell. Although what WE see takes priority in our growth, what others see helps us to determine if we're on track. In this regard, the opinion of others does matters on our journey but not in the sense of trying to people-please or become who someone else thinks we should be. In an effort to become a better version of yourself, work on actively aligning your words with your actions and the image in which you desire to be displayed consistently.

For one whole day, put yourself together from head to toe. Intentionally dress, act, and respond the way you see yourself. Pay attention to everything that comes out of *your* mouth and everything *you* do. This will open the door for a true self-evaluation and will help you to better understand why people see you the way they do. (Think before you speak. Think before you act.)

Now let's take things a step further. The following assignment, when properly executed, will increase your overall awareness.

Exercise D:

Choose a small group of 3-5 people and speak with them individually (one on ones are highly suggested here to avoid feeing double-teamed or attacked). Engage them in positive, neutral, and negative zone topics, and try to be completely open and receptive to their answers. During this live exercise, practice maintaining a positive or neutral facial expression with a straight posture and a closed mouth. You should not defend yourself or give feedback while they are speaking. After their response to each question/statement, you absolutely must not play the victim. Doing so will justify any negative behavior they may have relayed to you while closing the door for growth and change. If you do this, you will remain in the same state you were in before attempting this exercise. Instead you should simply say, "I understand," while honestly seeking understanding. You can ask them questions to help you gain a better understanding as to why they see you in this light, such as, "Can you tell me what I do that brings you to this conclusion?" or "When do these behaviors/responses occur?" These are important questions because you may not be aware of specific behaviors that led them to seeing you this way, and they help you to get to know yourself through the eyes of others. If they are giving you positive feedback it is just as important to have the same questions answered: ("Can you tell me what I do that brings you to this conclusion?" or "When do these behaviors/responses occur?") because these may be strengths upon which you can maximize. Feedback is critical, but keep in mind that no one's responses should define you; their responses are there to give you insight, and your responses to their feedback **is** very important.

How to know you're not who you think you are? Pay very close attention to yourself during this assessment. Are you activating your power to grow? Don't go in expecting the good, don't go in expecting the bad; go in expecting the truth.

Exercise E:

POSITIVE / NEUTRAL / NEGATIVE ZONE

Engage your selected 3-5 individuals in the activity below:

The Zone you choose to start with is ultimately up to you. Based on my own focus group testing, I have found that starting with the neutral zone can sometimes lead to covering all zones; however, based on your personality type, you may want to either start with the positive zone or choose one question/statement from each category to balance the responses. The goal is to go through each zone completely and to come out with a clear view of your strengths and weaknesses.

POSITIVE ZONE:

These questions are directly seeking a positive response.

- As an employer/friend/co-worker/partner/sibling etc. ... what attracts you to me?
- What are three things about me that motivate you?
- What is one thing you think I am really good at?
- What do you like most about me?

NEUTRAL ZONE:

These questions/statements are solely seeking the person's views about you.

- Describe how you see me. (This can be the icebreaker for all zones.)
- What do you think about my appearance?
- What do I contribute to society?

- How would you describe my personality?
- Name something that I am consistent at doing. (Here you can be more specific. Ask about something you consistently do that is viewed as a good or bad thing.)
- Are there any qualities about me you wish you could have?
- What do you think other people think of me?
- How do I respond when other people around me are complimented?
- How do I react when I don't get what I want?
- How comfortable are you around me when I am unhappy?

NEGATIVE ZONE:

These questions/statements are seeking what the person believes you need to work on.

- Name one thing you think I can do differently that will make me a better person.
- If I could change one thing that could positively impact my overall character, what would it be?
- Is there anything I do that annoys you?
- What is my worst attribute? What do I need to work on the most?
- Why do you believe I struggle with in these areas?

These kinds of questions/statements are simple and direct. Although some may seem repetitive, they should lead to open dialogue that may go beyond the question, which will give you a complete idea of how others view you. Some people will see you in different lights based on their levels of interaction with you. There may even be an instance when two or more people tell you the same things. If this is the case, make sure to document where you are consistent, be it good or bad.

- Ask yourself what has to change in order for you to become who you are meant to be. What do you have to give up in order to free yourself from the things that are holding you back? At the end of this exercise you should be able to look at who you say you are and who others believe you are and have a clearer picture of who you may really be. Do not be alarmed if who you are on paper does not match the feedback you were given. It is imperative for you to know the differences because these things are important factors in your ability to shine.

- Take the positive feedback and focus on the strengths and favorable responses people shared with you. These are going to be your inner allies and can be used on your behalf to work as undercover change agents. Use them to combat the negatives whenever they show up. For example, if someone told you one of the things you do to annoy them is procrastinate or take no initiative, but one of your positive attributes is being effective when completing an assignment, if asked to do something, don't just do it effectively, think about the things you need to work on such as procrastination and make a point to do what they've asked you in a timely manner. It may feel unpleasant because you are being stretched beyond your comfort zone, but the benefit of incremental change is to help you become both reliable and consistent, which enhances your character attributes. Think about what you need to work on but focus on what you are good at. Use your strengths to outshine your weaknesses.

The only way your allies will work on your behalf is if you actively combat the issues in the Negative Zone daily, moment by moment, until they begin to fade. To maintain awareness, take the initiative to check yourself when going about your day. In every activity, ask yourself if you are giving your best. This is not to put you in a negative mindset; its purpose is the complete opposite. That "above and beyond" piece is usually what gets people's recognition. (Awareness is something that obviously wasn't present in the Negative Zone, and the only way to combat those issues is by acknowledging and addressing them.)

While taking this deep look at yourself, keep in mind that it is important that you not turn the focus on anyone else. This process is for you to see you, not for you to point out the flaws in others while addressing your own. Those around you can go through this process on their own accord; this process is most effective when done as a solo journey. Why? Because what you find should not be influenced by what someone else is learning, going through, or dealing with as a result of seeing him or herself.

The people you chose to assist you in this exercise are not the enemy. Remember, you asked them to be honest; do not spite them for telling you things that could have potentially held you back from your best. Sure, they also have things to work on; otherwise there would be a class of flawless people out there, but there aren't. If they did not have the courage to tell you the truth, you would more than likely remain a dim-lit bulb. Whatever you believe about yourself is true, but if you are unwilling to grow, that truth will remain in your eyes only.

So how do you get other people to see you the way you do? Take action. Action equals change, and the best way to change is to practice. My mother shared a story with me that was once shared with her. *A little girl told her mother she wanted to be a ballerina; her mother bought her some ballerina shoes and a tutu and told her to practice*! There's nothing deep about this story until it is applied to your life. There are two steps: equip yourself, and then take action. You can wear the costume of who or what you want to become, but until you actively take the necessary and repetitive steps of learning, practicing and repeating, you will remain in a wanting state of mind. To practice is to do something over and over until you become better at it. This exercise is about you and your response to the things around you that you have no control over. You do, however, have control over your responses. Essentially, practice equals positioning yourself for what you want.

ACCEPTANCE AND KEEPING IT MOVING

I have been told by several people in my personal life that I could have more patience in my response to forgetful people. I know that in order for me to overcome this, I must spend more time in the presence of absent-minded people and practice patience until I become better at responding accordingly. As a life coach this is important to me. I would not want to lack patience with someone who needs me.

In order for you to be seen in the light in which you desire to stand, you have to accept the truth about yourself and constantly work on areas that need improvement. If you are uncertain as to whether or not you need to take the time to See Yourself, I have outlined several characteristics that speak directly to someone who may.

- You have lost more than five jobs, contracts, or internships within a two- to three-year period.
- If you are an employer, you have a high turnover of staff and/or multiple complaints from employees. (Recommendation: Do an anonymous SWAT analysis if you want to know how your staff views you). In this case, try not to focus so much on figuring out who said what rather than what was said. The point is to address what has been said in order to create a quality product (YOU).
- You keep dating the same person (personality/quality-wise) over and over again but take no accountability for your actions when things don't work out. (There is a lesson here, and until you get it you cannot move on. You will continue to meet and date the same person. Do not blame them as the problem. The problem is that your lesson has not yet been learned and there is more than likely something in you that needs to be addressed.)
- You have more than two difficult relationships simultaneously (with relatives, friends, spouse, siblings, co-workers, etc.). (It is not a horrible thing to have difficult relationships; people can be difficult. What you have to look for here are two things. Do you have multiple difficult relationships consistently, and do these difficult relationships rotate, meaning is it with two people this month, a different set of people three months from now, etc.? Either way this needs to be addressed, but these are two different issues. If you have two or more difficult relationships with the same people over the course of time, forgiveness may need to be addressed here. If your difficult relationships rotate, whereas you always have them but with different

people, take a long hard look at yourself and the pattern as to why this is a consistent part of your life. Some of these people need to be in your 3-5 in order for you to gain clarity.)

- People constantly say things about you that you do not believe are true.
- Someone keeps telling you the same negative thing about yourself over the course of a year, and nothing has changed.
- You are angry in your spirit and don't know why.
- You seem like a target for negative things.
- You put lots of energy in trying to make things right but the results do not reflect it.
- Your circle of friends is small by default and not by choice. (You don't have to have a large group of friends; the key words here are "by default," meaning you have a hard time maintaining friendships.)
- Different people who have nothing to do with each other respond to you in the same negative way.
- You have a snappy attitude and accept it as a part of your personality.
- You are always frustrated.
- You complain daily.
- You do an amazing job at work but have never been promoted, acknowledged, or given a merit increase. (I recommend initiating a conversation with your employer. This could be due to an oversight, your wardrobe, actions, a lack of company funds, etc. ... but you need to know. The more you can define yourself, the better you can shine.)
- People cringe in your presence.
- You are constantly ill but have no documented deficiency, nor have you been diagnosed with an ailment.
- You always have to be right or have the last word.
- You jump to conclusions and are often proven wrong.

- You consistently interrupt people when they are speaking. (Your thoughts are no more important than theirs. If you are interrupting to avoid forgetting what you want to say, take notes and refer back to them once the other person has completed his or her thought.)
- You are driven to enter relationships based on looks. (The outer appearance represents roughly 25% of what you will get from a person in a relationship; choosing based on looks will often lead to disappointment.)
- You take jobs with the mindset that you are only there to collect a paycheck or until what you really want comes along.
- You feel that people are not on your level. (There's only one level, h*uman*.)
- You intentionally fill your time with things that do not promote where you are trying to go and who you strive to become (gossip, video clips of youth fighting, or so-called funny videos of mentally challenged individuals, pornography, etc.). (There is nothing wrong with entertainment, but try not to water down what you stand for or your beliefs by what the media makes easily accessible to you.)
- You constantly compare yourself to others. (The only way to shine is to take your eyes off of others and intently fix them on yourself. What you have to offer shines beyond the lights around you.)
- You have the ability to work and choose not to. (Work is a broad word. Although you may not work a 9-5 or be a business owner, you can do work around your home, volunteer, mentor, and so on. If you are not employed or self-employed and are not taking care of a child/children, the idea of not working doesn't cut it. If you have the physical and mental ability to work, you should be currently and actively doing so; otherwise, ask yourself, "What am I doing? What do I contribute to society? What do I expect out of life?")

- You leave a trail of damaged relationships. (Ask yourself this: "Am I relationship poor or wealthy?")
- You copy specific things about people in hopes of getting a similar response from others instead of tapping into your own identity. (Be unique; be you.)
- You have a hard time celebrating the success of others. (Openly or secretly, this only hinders you from reaching the peak of your own success.)
- You are a serial dater. (You find yourself in and out of relationships with different people, or you find yourself dating person after person and/or multiple people at once. Ask yourself, "Why am I really doing this? What am I looking for? What do I ultimately want? With this behavior, are you setting yourself up to receive what you want?" Being young or just because you're single is not the answer to either of these questions.)
- You justify bad choices.
- You intentionally push others' buttons to get the reaction you desire.
- You add no value to the people in your life.
- You see no value in time. (Procrastination only steals from your life.)
- You struggle managing money even though you make enough to live off of.
- You are judgmental and easily point out the flaws in others.
- You invest in things that add no value to your life. (Where do you spend your time? Write down how your week looks from sun up to sun down and assess where you have the most time that can be used for your betterment.)
- You have low expectations (always expecting the worst in yourself and/or others). (This is dangerous because you get what you put out.

If this negative energy is what you believe in, you will get what you expect as a result of the energy you feed.)

- You see yourself, recognize that you need to change, and continue to make the same bad choices. (Now there is a chance that you see yourself, and there is not much change required. However, if you are being honest with yourself and others have expressed the need for change in you, and you choose to take no positive action, you are choosing to limit your beautiful life.)
- You get joy out of causing division, havoc, drama, or confusion between people.
- You feel vindicated in telling someone off.
- You live a dishonest lifestyle.
- Your motives are for the demise of others.

Whether or not any of the above-mentioned characteristics speak to you, I encourage you to complete the following exercise.

Exercise F:

- Write down how you see yourself after assessing yourself through the eyes of others. Does it differ from what you originally saw?
- How do you want to see yourself?
- How do you want to be seen?
- Envision how you want to see yourself using positive affirmations to solidify what you see.

ENVISIONING THE FUTURE YOU DESIRE

Do you have a concrete vision for your life? Sometimes we have a vision in our mind but we only think about it when it is relevant. What does it look like? Think about your vision in categories. How is it concerning your relationship with God, with others, in your career, with your finances, in your love life, in relation to personal growth, and so on?

Keep in mind that vision is all about seeing things bigger than they are right now, but it doesn't have to be far-fetched. Your vision can start with what you want tomorrow to look like or what your life looks like a year from now.

Write a vision statement for your life:

I wake up at 7 a.m. to the smell of fresh roasting coffee. I walk into the kitchen and see my Aunt Jackie standing on her own for the first time in three years. Her legs are in perfect condition. She turns from the stove and hands me my favorite mug filled with her famous coffee. We sit on the back porch and laugh for hours as she shares her childhood stories with me. I leave her on the porch and go into the study to finish writing a children's book I've been working on for two years. I complete it within hours...

This is an example of what a next-day vision statement can look like. Keep writing it until you cover all the details of your journey. This is similar to a short-term goal but can also be broken down into affirmations. You are drawing the things you desire to you with your thoughts and words by putting them on paper. And yes, your vision can include other people. I encourage you to only include people in your vision if the two of you are in agreement with their role in your vision (Matthew 18:19). When writing your vision make sure not to compare yourself with anyone else or you will lower your standards and limit yourself. No one is better than you; you are working on accessing the things in your life that make you as great as things you can only imagine for yourself. You are your own limitation, just as your current situation is your own motivation.

Writing how you see yourself gives your vision life and power. Once you have written your short- or long-term vision statement, turn it into an outline of goals, and then let your words and actions continue to reflect what you see. The clearer you are on your dream list, and the more you add to it, the more your vision evolves. Over time, the goals you derive from your vision should be moving. If they aren't, you may want to simplify them. If one of your goals is to write a book, instead of listing the goal as to write a book, consider the details of what that really looks like. In what genre are you writing, will research be required, what days and times will you commit to writing, will you self-publish or seek a publishing house, are you a new writer and will you attend writing workshops beforehand?

Be realistic about your vision, but also be fearless. Allow nothing to limit what you want to see come to fruition in your life.

When you begin to really see yourself, don't be afraid to love that person. If for any reason you don't like what you see, keep in mind that you have the power to change. There is no one else who shares your exact thoughts, ideas, ways, emotions, or way of digesting information. You are special whether you want to be or not, and you have something no one else in this world has. Do your best to be completely open to change because you only have the ability to achieve what you allow your mind to receive. Repeat these words. "I AM so naturally powerful that all I have to do is invest in myself to ignite every ability that lives inside me to achieve everything I want."

SHINE

You have purpose! You were created to fulfill a mission no one else can achieve but you. You are far more important than your environment. No matter what you see, what you are going through, or who is speaking against you, keep going! Never dull your shine for the sake of someone else's ego. You were created to be far more than what your thoughts are limited to. Limited meaning, whatever you can imagine, God has greater in mind for you. Why does God want more from you? Because He knows what you're capable of, you just have to believe you are as good as He sees you. To see yourself is to be as self-aware as possible. To know who you are in any situation and to gain the ability to think before you speak and act. Think about the outcome, the consequences; imagine if what you say or do is being said or done to you. Are you aware of the limitless person trapped inside of you? To shine is not a surface ability. What you look like, wear, or have do not allow you to shine at all. Nuclear fusion makes the sun shine by turning hydrogen into helium in its core. Become familiar with your core, your creator, your why, your true self. The power in shining is not knowing these things; the power comes from your activation of these things. Many of us fear the knowing, assuming it will prevent us from being happy, doing what we want or having fun. The truth is, the reveling in this allows us to have everything we want from the inside out. You were not created to be a dim-lit bulb. You were created to shine! It's a process, and it starts from the inside.

AFFIRMATIONS

Here I am God, this is me. I'm not where I want to be and I need you to show me who I am. I realize that knowing myself allows me the wisdom to see what you put inside me.

CHAPTER 2

Have Confidence

What does confidence look like? For many people confidence is based on the essentials of appearance, possessions, wealth, and access; for others, not so much. Regardless of what area in life in which we are working to build our confidence, the common denominator is information. What don't we know, what can't we anticipate, why can't we accept rejection, and so on? Typically, we would like to know the outcome of anything we attempt outside of our comfort zone before we try. There is a scripture in the Bible that says, "Seek and ye shall find", read (Mathew 7:7-8). What are we seeking? Information—facts about something or someone. When we have information, it builds our trust in that something or someone, including self. Spiritually, in Christianity, when we seek to know who God/Jesus is through His Word, both our understanding and confidence in Him also grow. This then births faith and trust in His ability to achieve all things in our lives through His provisions.

Can I trust your response to my output—whether it is by how I look or speak, what I know about a certain topic, etc.? Many of us require positive responses from people to play a big part in how confident we feel while others could care less. One thing that will certainly work to build anyone's confidence is what the person believes he or she knows about something, even in relationships. Have you ever dated someone who you knew for certain would not cheat on you? How at ease were you to travel out of town for work knowing you could trust that person? Imagine carrying that feeling with you in every area, from what you drive or however you get around, to your appearance, your ability to do your job, manage money, approach people you don't know in an effort to network, and so on. The comfort you have or had that allowed you to trust this person is there because you believe you know him or her. To know something or someone is to have information. Having information builds trust and ultimately confidence.

Create a list of affirmations that speak to what you believe and recite them regularly. What tends to help people who have a hard time initiating their own confidence is having someone else speak into them. Whether you are someone who has a strong sense of confidence or not, practice positively affirming other people. This too comes back to you in the areas you may need it most. An affirmation can be viewed as a compliment or a forward-speaking claim. If you have a friend who is a great dancer and dreams of performing on Broadway, encourage them, affirm them verbally by saying how amazing they are and how nothing will stop their dream. When we hear affirmations from others, it gives us the courage to continue our pursuits. All it takes is for us to believe we are good at something for confidence to show up.

Have you ever been told, "You're powerful?" You are. Power is ability, capacity, competence, and potential. You have the power to create. What we begin in our thought-life implants itself into our reality. Create the life you want, one thought and one accomplishment at a time. Understand that with a vision and time, every small step matters. You may not have confidence in every area of your life, but you can and will in the areas you target. To have the ability to go after something and get it leaves us feeling empowered. This is why it is important to finish what we start. If you struggle with believing in yourself, now is the time to figure out why. Is there something from your past holding you back? Do you feel as though you need to see something happen before you will believe that greater things are not only coming but are already here? Do you feel like your personality stops you from getting better results? Confidence is important when it comes to who you think you are and who you want to become. It can be very hard to see things go well for others and stagnate for you, but the worst thing you can do is build a home in that space. Instead, turn your attention to the areas *you* need to focus on. Your focus should be intently set on unlocking what is inside of you so that you can attain the things you desire. We all have a Purpose, a Place, and a Plan that will ultimately come together. The quality of your journey will be dictated by your ability to see yourself, have confidence, and, if nothing else, have an idea for the vision for your life. Keep in mind that a vision is not a complete picture; it is the seed of direction. Have faith in your life vision. There may not be a grand sign that solidifies your vision, but trust that it is already inside you. Seek it and it will come out.

The feedback you received in Chapter one, both positive and negative, will assist you with confidence building. The positive feedback should be listed as affirmations, and the negative feedback should only be placed in your thoughts in conjunction with ideas on how you can improve in these areas. You can also turn the negative feedback into counteractive affirmations. If someone said you exaggerate the truth, you would affirm, *'I tell the truth without exaggerating'.* What people think of you should not dictate how you see yourself; it should only be used as a guide that allows you to assess what you're putting out there for people to see. Different people will have different views about you based on the time they've spent in your presence.

In 2014, I had a speaking engagement at a women's conference in Nashville, TN. One of the women at the event became someone I am still very close to today. In fact, she took me on for a period of time as her life coach. In one of our first phone conversations she said, "You could be intimidating." I paused at first and thought to myself, *what does that mean to her and what did I do to leave that impression?*

When I asked what made her think that, she said, "When you were speaking, you came off very sure about yourself. You seemed to know what you were talking about, and you were very confident." I asked if that was a good or bad thing in her eyes.

She replied, "No, it's definitely a good thing. I wasn't intimidated by you, but someone who isn't as strong in their business mindset may have been."

She had no idea how nervous I get every time I have to speak in front of people. I'm almost shaking inside before I go on any stage or stand before a crowd, but I always say a prayer right before I open my mouth. Regardless of whether I stutter, speak too fast, or say "um" too many times, I ask for the wisdom and courage to shine. Shine meaning, show up, deliver, attract people, leave them with something they can use, and be unforgettable! After the conversation with this woman I had to ask myself, *is this how I want people to see me when I speak?* The answer is "yes." Not only do I want to appear confident, but I also want people to believe that I know what I am talking about on any topic I prepare for. Isn't this the whole point of studying one's craft? To deliver. I asked her in spite of that, what attracted her to me. She said it was the warmth of my personality. Asking the right questions helped me understand a stranger's point of view. The take-away from this is not to focus so much on how others see us and what they think about us; it is for us to become more aware of who we are outside of what we think. *When it comes to actions, reality will always trump a daydream.*

There was another instance when I was coaching a mentee, and she told me she wanted to have a refocusing session so she could improve her marketing strategy at work, learn how to control/dominate a conversation, find balance, and build her confidence. I addressed three out of four of her concerns. Balance is something we would have to revisit after she began to work on the other areas, which again boiled down to information. If I were asked to speak on a topic I had no knowledge about, my confidence level would not be as high until or unless I studied the information from the root up. Information is one side of it, but what if she had to deliver it in front of other people; that would be another area we would have to work on building confidence. In her case, she wouldn't have to deliver in front of a crowd, but she did have to share information with customers, which can be just as frightening. Her problem was that she didn't understand certain terms, nor did she understand the "WHY" behind some of the decisions her boss made when she'd shadow him while dealing with customers. Do you believe that if she understood all of the terms and processes of her job that she would be confident in leading a conversation with a customer? Absolutely! Knowing the information about a product you're selling has just as much to do with the successful outcome of a sale as personality does. When you can answer questions and give explanations, people value you as a resource. A light went on inside of her that will carry her through building the confidence she needs through studying, creating a marketing strategy, and leading conversations with customers on her own. One of the easiest roads to confidence is self-development. This goes back to what the woman in Nashville saw in me. Not only was I certain about what I delivered to that group of women, but I also spent time on my appearance and hygiene, my tone, energy and eye contact—all of which painted a picture of confidence in her eyes. *I am what I say I am, I am what I put energy and effort into.* It's the effort we put into the total package of mastering our craft that will take us to higher heights.

TIPS FOR NEW SPEAKERS, PRESENTERS, TEACHERS & CONSULTANTS:

When speaking be clear, and when you dress make sure you are comfortable. Wear what makes you feel good. Clothes that have to be adjusted as you present, sell, recruit, pitch, or share can be distracting to the person(s) you are selling yourself to. You are always selling yourself first and then your product or service. If people like you, they may buy into your service solely based on who you are. Cleanliness is important because the opposite can be a very distracting turn-off. Also, connect with the audience. Whether one person or a hundred people, it is as important to focus on them as much as what you are trying to get them to buy into. This is not just for work relationships. These tips are character building and can help you improve in every relationship.

Just like presenting a quality product to someone shopping for a luxury item, you have to present yourself the way you see yourself far beyond the current moment. If you are a school secretary but you see yourself becoming the principal of the school, present the qualities of a principal now. Having confidence in who you believe you are requires a genuine *you* no matter what that looks like. Why is confidence important in shining in our lane? Because confidence is attractive. Not only to other people but more so to opportunities that are out there designed specifically for you. When people see that you are sure of your abilities their need for you in that area automatically increases. Believe you can shine and you will. If you believe you cannot, you won't. Many of the speaking engagements I've had in the past came from someone hearing me speak or hearing about me, and topics I've shared. I am not the best speaker in the world; there are thousands if not millions of great speakers out there, but I am confident in the energy I bring, my ability to relate to and connect with people, and the wisdom I have been blessed to share with others. These are the things that give me the courage to have confidence no matter who goes before or after me. I am my greatest competition; you are your greatest competition. All we have to do is be better than we were the last time around to outshine ourselves, and that takes practice.

How do I sharpen my tools? I study my craft, read, be open to what my mentors have to say but maintain the discernment to know what applies to me, and I consistently walk in faith, pushing myself beyond my comfort zone in an effort to reach my next level. This means sometimes doing things I don't want to do or feel like doing but understanding how they apply to and affect me overall. This is my system thinking in action. If you do not have a system, consider making a list of action steps that can be applied to your thought-life to make your daydreams reality.

REAL VALUE: CONFIDENCE UP CLOSE

This system can be altered and applied to different areas and relationships. Consider your work life and then your home life, keeping in mind that it's *all* life. I worked in corporate America for many years and I encountered a few people who would make excuses for their behavior at work by saying, "*I'm not like this outside of work*" or "*This place makes me like this.*" I would always tell myself, "I beg to differ." I say that because life is life and who we are in one setting cannot be erased just because we say so. It's important that we adopt a system of thinking that compliments who we want to be. Once we practice this system daily, it eventually becomes a natural part of who we are and allows us to have and exude confidence. Whether these relationships are between you and your mother, father, sibling, friend, co-worker, business partner, spouse, employer, or anyone else, there is a formula for you. I wasn't able to create my own until I went through these chapters in my own life. These chapters taught me how to separate the necessary from the unnecessary things.

Things and status have the ability to drive one's ego, leading to cockiness, but *things and status* also have the ability to cause a lack of confidence. When it comes to where you live, what you drive, how much money you have or make, what you look like, what you wear, who you know, and what you've been exposed to, none of this should make or break you as a person. Why? Because all of these things can change. We have to shift our mindsets to a place where we choose confidence based on who we know we are in our core and where we believe we are going by discovering our authentic self. Your biggest asset is the one who stares back at you in the mirror. What is it that you want to achieve? If you dress up, comb your hair, and put on a fragrance, when you look in the mirror, how do you feel? The answer is probably something positive because of the effort you put into your appearance. Ask yourself how you would feel if you groomed your inside the same way. The bottom line is that you get what you put out. This applies to *every* area of your life. The people around you are a reflection of you—your energy, your words and actions, and anything else you put out. There is at least one thing a person around you has in common with you that lured them to you in the first place. The attraction can even be the desire they have to be more like the character they see in you.

The purpose here is to examine what you release so you can understand what you are attracting and why. This is important because it applies to everything from money to opportunities, to relationships. Have you ever met a person who at first glance was not physically your type but after being in their presence all you could think about was seeing them again? Self-confidence can make a person attractive because what attracts us is not really their appearance at all. Looks are the first thing we are introduced to when meeting new people, but what is beneath the exterior is what will make a person stay or leave, invite you back, make an investor crack open their wallet, or even make an employer choose you over all of the other qualified people in your field who appear to have the same thing to offer. Personality helps expose our level of confidence. Working inward-out is how you shine, so remember that you matter more than any material thing you possess. The real you is not what is seen with the eyes, it's what's beneath the shell that people see when they meet you, which is tied to their vision based on the glimpse of what you show them. True confidence is not confused with cockiness and is not driven by things that come and go; it is a sureness of self, based on knowledge, inner strengths, beliefs, and the positive responses we get from others based on qualities that will never die, fade, or lose value.

THE WHOLE PERSON

As a coach, I see people in four aspects, each weighing 25%.

- The first is the shell, which is what you physically look like. It is solely based on appearance and is usually what initially attracts others if they have not yet been introduced to a different aspect of you.

53

- The second aspect is your core; who you are on the inside. This contains your life mission, vision, values, and beliefs—all of which dictate how you operate as a person and how you treat people.
- The third aspect is your personality, the qualities that make you, you. Quirks, habits, mannerisms, and how you interact with others and things.
- The fourth and last of these aspects is how you live. Are you organized and clean, do you cook or eat out, do you make a mess and leave it, is your car junky, etc.

Sometimes when we meet people and they only have our shell to go on, it can be tough to accept the fact that as they get to know us their feelings may change. Confidence can be built or shaken here simply based on a superficial encounter. Understand that it is not superficial for a person to determine their likability of you based on getting to know you and seeing that you are not what they had in mind, but it *is* superficial when we decide that we like, love, or care for someone solely based on their shell. Getting to know others should be what we all aim for in an effort to appropriately assess relationships. However, even before that, we should spend time getting to know ourselves. Choose the easy road and initiate this on your own. I know many people who through being broken, were forced into this by situation and not by choice.

Putting too much stock in the superficial is only the tip of the iceberg when it comes to destroying confidence. The most common threat to confidence is rejection. Yes, confidence often diminishes in the face of rejection. Think about a time when you asked for something that you really wanted and were told no, you attempted something and failed, or you believed something about yourself only to be proven the contrary by someone whose opinion you valued. These can all be direct hits to your level of confidence, but instead of letting them destroy it, use them as lamps to your path. Consider these responses to be moments when the light has been turned on in a dark room. Now that you have been enlightened to the fact you will not always get the response you want, use this awareness to take the initiative to assess the why behind the response. This does not mean for you to harass anyone or to keep asking for or doing the same thing over and over. It simply means, you now realize there is work to do to get what you want. When you self-assess and try again, you are subconsciously building your confidence. Ultimately, along with knowledge, understanding is also a part of this journey. If you lack understanding you will spin your wheels and attain no traction. Pay attention to the details in your output, ask questions to gain a better perspective when uncertain, and create a thought system that contributes to the growth of the ultimate you.

In fact, being the ultimate you—whole and confident—is valuable in more ways than you may think. Confidence creates wealth and opportunities. For example, in a work environment, it can make employees feel secure about the longevity of the company, and it can make a boss trust a staff member they barely know. In business, confidence can attract people to your company and show clients and colleagues that you know what you're doing. With the ability to sell yourself without words, true confidence can make people buy into you, your product or service and, in some cases, just so they can possess something that you have to increase their confidence. *By sharing the air of greatness, I too become great.*

Even in a relationship, you should strive to be as confident about yourself as possible. How do we gain this mystery amount of confidence to help develop into our shine? By seeing, knowing, and accepting

55

ourselves completely, by allocating time to the areas in our lives that need to be addressed, and by actively seeking and participating in personal development. As we enhance the whole person, confidence has no choice but to blossom. Have you ever known so much about something that no one could shake the confidence you had in that thing? Imagine knowing yourself to that same degree. The sun knows why it shines and it does so from its core; so should you.

Now consider, none of us were meant to do life alone. As we focus on ourselves, the mission is really to be in position for those around us. How would it feel if you knew you could count on others to be in position when your time to shine arrived? To know that if you stepped off a cliff, the people who are designated to be your net are in position to catch you and build a bridge for your next step. The more time we all spend on improving our inner selves, the more confident we are to walk into our purpose, which happens to be tied to someone else's, and someone else's.

SHINE

Live out who you want to be through faith. Dwell only on the things that will make you greater now and let them carry you to the next step in your path. You can begin to build your confidence by surrounding yourself with confident people, doing your best to finish what you start, and learning how take compliments without talking yourself out of them. Stop taking away from your abilities and remember the power of affirmations. We constantly learn new things about ourselves as we grow. Read (Jeremiah 17:7) and know that it is okay to put your confidence in God if you struggle with gaining confidence in yourself.

AFFIRMATIONS

I vie to see myself through your eyes as I develop a sureness of self-worth and unquestionable value. I am confident in your ability to use me. I am confident.

CHAPTER 3

Ignite Your Inner Strength

Where does inner strength come from? Our core. We all have a source of power that gives us the ability to exert confidence, accomplish a goal that appears to be unrealistic, and keep going when everything around us tells us to quit. Knowing you have purpose provides an avenue to your inner strength.

A lackluster environment or negative occurrences can be detractors designed to cloud your vision and prevent you from reaching into this power source.

I've learned that what allows me to tap into my inner strength is the action connected to faith. "Faith without works is dead" (James 2:17). Because I have a vision and am a believer, I know that I cannot make the life I want happen without effort. I also cannot do it all on my own. I do what I have the ability to with faith that God will meet me where I am, and He does. Whatever it is that I believe, faith gives me the drive to take action towards what I want in an effort to attain it. Wherever you are on your life journey, God will meet you there. Whatever you lack in ability, understanding, or wherever your capabilities end—His grace, favor, and provisions dwell in that space. For this reason, even when things look bleak, you *must* keep going.

FIND YOUR TRIGGER

Some people in my industry may use music to get them pumped up, a phone call from a loved one, a sentimental item they carry with them, a memory, meditation, etc. The idea is to become familiar with what triggers strength inside of you when you need it. If in a relationship, consider what makes you confident in your role. Is it words of affirmation from your mate, being able to take care of them, feeling secure in your commitment? At work, are you most confident when your ideas are implemented, when your customers leave positive feedback, or when your boss or staff give you praise? If you are a parent, are you most confident when a friend compliments the way you raise your children, when your mate tells you how good you look, or when you witness someone's response to how you manage your home? We all know at least one thing that makes us feel confident; we just have to learn how to activate confidence on our own. And just like we have to learn how to direct negative or positive energy, we have to also learn how to ignite or direct our strengths. When we focus on our strengths, we have less time to dwell on imperfections and more time to shine through our positive attributes.

We all believe in something, but the firmness of that belief is often what gets us through experiences. Whether it's inner strength, natural strength, or physical strength, they each have a source. My inner strength is evident to anyone who knows me. I often say in reference to God that I am nothing but a speck of dust on the bottom of a shoe without Him, but with Him there is no limit in my life!

Natural strength comes from wisdom. Wisdom allows us to make better decisions regardless of what is taking place around us. It gives us the ability to rationalize and think things through to the end before taking certain actions. We all have different amounts of wisdom in different areas, but natural strength is a knowing that doesn't require research or extra efforts. It is having clarity about certain things and situations.

Physical strength is of course based on what you can do with your body. Many people work out in one way or another to build or maintain their physical strength for various reasons. This strength also refers to the body's ability to heal, reproduce, and grow.

Mental strength contributes to what we are able to deal with or accept in our thought life. Not to be confused with mental illness, mental strength here is referring to what you have control of (which is more than you probably think).

Inner, natural, and physical strength directly affect mental strength, and in turn, mental, natural, and physical strength are all derived from inner strength. What you believe, what you do, and what you *can* do are all tied to how you receive everything. Take some time to think about this. It is important to actively exercise all of these areas in an effort to ignite the strengths you may need to tap into on the spot. The more you work on your strengths, the more you can endure, and the more you will grow. How do you work on your areas of strengths? Focus. Give each of them undivided attention. For example: My mental strength is increased when I study, actively participate in personal development, read selected materials that stimulate my mind, and so on. My physical strength increases when I consistently use certain muscles such as walking my dog, going skating, or attending dance classes. My inner and natural strengths increase when I spend quiet time with God; pass integrity tests with work, family, friends, and in relationships; and how I respond to negative situations. What station is your mindset dialed in on? Choose the one(s) that will contribute most to who you are becoming.

IGNITE

Practice igniting each of these areas of strengths at different times. Once you see that you can do it, keep practicing. This has to be a conscious and consistent effort if you have a goal in mind. Do you want to lose weight, pass a test, start a business, move to a new city, or start a family? Whatever it is, it is possible. Remember, a thought accompanied by an action equals the possibility of whatever it is that you desire. Desires are tied to our inner strength because we are naturally built to achieve what we desire. When we want something, a trigger inside of us immediately begins to map a plan on how to attain it. Some desires are derived from what we take in (which are not necessarily natural, but manufactured by things we expose ourselves to or allow in our ear and eye gates) such as violence, the demise of others, adultery, pornographic images, etc.

Inner strengths are like idle weapons, by existence alone they have no power, but if used properly can be quite impactful, both powerful and even fearful. Have you ever seen a glimpse of what you are capable of and received so much praise and acknowledgement for it that it frightened you to know that you really are unstoppable? That this one simple thing required so little for you to be seen in such a great light! In that moment you were being vetted by your shine. Did you know that what is in you is silently waiting to be activated? You don't have to waste your time sizing up invisible competition. To activate your strengths, simply act, speak, and do. If you need the courage to move forward, start off small. Pick something as simple as making a phone call you've been avoiding. Tell yourself that you will be humble, nonthreatening, and that you will listen well. Believe that no matter what, at the end of that call everything will be all right. Control your emotions and feel free to accept responsibility for any misunderstanding that may occur. At the end of the call you will have tapped into your inner strength. Once you've accomplished something like this, have confidence that you can take the next step and then the next. If the ultimate fear in life is the loss of life, then what do you have to lose by moving yours in the right direction? We have to free our minds in order to release vision and power. These are important factors in igniting our strengths. See it! Believe it! Say it! Receive it!

See it- Believe it

VISION

-VISION RELEASES POWER-

Say it- Receive it

POWER

There is one inner strength that is probably more important than all others: discernment. You may have heard someone say, "You need to have discernment," on the other end, someone is probably asking, "How do I get discernment?" or, "What is discernment?" Discernment is the ability to determine what you should do—or in other words, having good judgment. We all have different levels of discernment.

Discernment 101: The more time we spend in God's Word, the better prepared we are to judge situations (not people). Whatever you have the ability to do with your hands from writing to building things, what would the outcome be if you spent ten minutes writing a book, or fifteen minutes building a house? Would there not be a difference if you spent adequate time on either of these? This is what it's like when we spend time with God. You can have a conversation with someone and never mention His name, but people can since your invested time with Him based on the vibrations from within you. During quiet times He is imparting in you the secrets of how to deal with situations that have not yet happened in your life. There are great stories in the Bible that give us examples of what to expect and how to react. When people do things out of character and remove themselves from my life in a business or personal setting, I always look for God. I assess the situation by referring back to what I want, what I've asked for, and who I've prayed for to determine if any of those things are taking place based on what's happening. If you want to be elevated, prepare to lose people, but maintain your integrity. Accept the changes that are required for your path's journey and don't give away your reputation by getting into verbal or physical altercations with bugs on your windshield. Try not to dwell on what someone did rather than reflect on what needs to take place next. If you've asked God to remove people from your life that don't belong and replace them with people who need you, or are meant to accompany you on your journey, you can't question when someone never returns your call or a friend decides to become an enemy. You also can't hold it against the people who must be used to propel you. Maybe your co-workers who once loved you are now working against you in an effort to get you fired because you asked God for a promotion. That promotion may be with another company. Maybe the person you've loved for years decided to cheat on you because you told God you were ready for marriage. He or she is more than likely not the mate He had in mind for you, and maybe this took place so that you would have the ability to openly recognize the person He designed for you.

What makes more sense? Spending time trying to figure out why someone did something, or spending time seeking understanding and accepting the fact that God may have allowed the enemy to use these people to fulfill a prayer request? Our plans are not His plans, our thoughts are not His thoughts and our ways are not His ways. In my reality, I realize that I cannot help everyone, and some people are not meant to be tied to one another even if they are both good people. Eventually we have to learn how to look for, and see God in every situation. He is our ultimate strength.

SHINE

Inner strength is an essential element that often stands amidst the levels in which you currently are and those you are capable of achieving. For every challenge or obstacle we face, there is also a way around or through it, pause and read (Genesis 22:11-14). Let nothing within your control stand between you reaching your full potential. If you had any idea how powerful you are, you just might be more excited than afraid. The greatest of us all is the one who is self-aware and uses that awareness as a positive tool to help ourselves and those around us. To effectively apply inner strength you must have understanding. Understanding allows you to apply different strengths to different areas. Does this mean inner strength is a magic pill that will fix all of your problems? No, it's a tool that can assist you during the pitfalls on your journey. Each of us has a way of processing information. How we apply our strengths does not matter as much as our ability to know when to apply them. Find a quiet place to have quiet time with the source of your core.

AFFIRMATIONS

The more I connect with you (God), the more I realize I can do all things through the strength you have given me. I see now the secret of pushing past difficult times and how it allows me to soar beyond any limitation in my path.

CHAPTER 4

No Negative Self-Talk

If I am truly made in the image of God, does this mean I have similar abilities? Yes. If you want to understand the influence your words have over your life and those around you, here it is in a nutshell. (Genesis 1:3), "Then God said, '*Let there be light,*' and there was light." It's that simple. God's word is foundation. How are you building and shaping the foundation of your life? When you *will* something to yourself with your words, don't be surprised when you get it. Just like people are attracted to certain energies others put out, so are your thoughts connected to things. We think it, say it, and receive it. If you don't have money and you say, "I'm broke," what is the difference between you saying *that* and receiving it, and God saying "Let there be light," and there's light? There is no difference.

Negative self-talk is birthed through you, in a realm where your thoughts and ability to accept marry. In this scenario, 'broke' is more likely to become your reality than wealth by the hand of your own affirmation. Not Tim who owes you money and not Amy who could have given you a better reference for that higher-paying job. Not even the people who talked negatively to or about you your whole life. There have been times when I had less than lunch money in my pocket for longer than a week, but I did not receive 'broke' as my (then) *current state of being*. My words reflected where I saw myself and I repeated them until I arrived at that place. "*All of my needs are met, I have more than enough money to take care of myself, my family and give to others. My overflow increases as I give and money is not an issue, concern, or lord in my life. Money is attracted to me."* I was so specific that I wrote down how much I wanted to earn daily, weekly, monthly, quarterly, and annually as well as how often I wanted to work, and the kind of work I wanted to do. During this process I would catch myself saying, *I can't afford this or that* every now and then, but my accountability partner would check me immediately. This is one of many areas in which I implemented the "no negative self-talk" rule in my life and my household.

Negative self-talk is so major that it has a pre-requisite, gossip. I know, you're just telling someone about something you witnessed or something that affected you in one way or another, right? Let's remember that when we put our words into action against someone else, it's just like applying NSF fees to our own checking account. What sense does that make? Why take away from your own good fortune by cursing someone's life while expecting blessings in yours. If you knew that when someone spoke against you it would cause a sort of lack in your life how would you feel? The power of words is as real as the encounter between your eyes and your mind as you read this book. If we were spoken into existence, and if we believe that if we ask for something we will receive it, then we must know that our words spoken over others have power in their lives, and vice versa. This is why there is an affirmative scripture to combat what others put out there against us, even if they don't understand what they are doing. (Isaiah 54:17), no weapon formed against me shall prosper.

I had the privilege of meeting a special person by the name of Roderick C. Ford many years ago. As I saw him in passing, he at times appeared to be talking to himself and he seemed to read a lot. What he was really doing was reciting affirmations, which he later taught me the depth of, and how to implement them in *my* daily routine. He gave me a printed copy that I sat next to my computer at work so I could gaze at them throughout my day; I even recited them in my car. Even though I had done them inconsistently here and there, I still wasn't ready to embrace them as a consistent part of my lifestyle. Sometimes we want to change, become better individuals, or implement positive consistencies in our lives but just aren't ready. A year had passed and I found myself writing new affirmations and putting them all over my bathroom mirror so I could look at them as I got dressed every day. Today I challenge myself by picking the first one my eyes land on and I practice repeating it throughout the day.

I've learned that when I want something, the easiest way <u>not</u> to get it is to tell myself I can't have it, or doubt my ability to receive it. My language has changed so much over the years that certain words or phrases are sharp and even offensive to hear such as: I can't pay my rent, I think all men are liars, everybody cheats, you can't get that job, or you aren't going to be successful if you work on more than one thing at a time. I curse these statements back to the black whole from whence they came. What we tell ourselves shapes us and our abilities. It is the plan of execution, the level of consistency, comprehension, and the ability to compartmentalize that equates to a good recipe for balance. One thing people often do without knowing it is limit your ability through what they believe about themselves, what they have been told by someone else, or past failed experiences. Everyone is built differently, but knowing yourself allows you to decide if you're someone who can only do one thing at a time, or if you can effectively multitask. There is no right or wrong to this; the key is to adopt what you know works successfully for you and not be limited by someone else's limitations. Receiving what people say to us is what makes those things our reality, which is why I often say out loud, "I don't receive that," to anything someone subconsciously puts out there as a definitive statement about me, my abilities, or my future that I disagree with. I do not believe in limiting God, and I have the discernment to keep reaching for what he built me for. This goes back to cursing people without knowing it. A curse doesn't always come across as something so pronounced that you are aware of it. Affirmations can be both positive and negative. If you do not have the money to pay your bills and you say it aloud, it may be a truth, but I recommend you saying, "I am not poverty-stricken; things may look like I am incapable of paying my rent, but all of my needs are met." Your words have the power to become your reality, and your power over the Universe shifts when you proclaim goodness over your life. Someone may show up and offer help, you may get that job you've waited months for, or even end up in a shelter where you find your purpose in helping others. I have a very close friend who lived in a homeless shelter with her kids when they were small due to domestic violence. Today she is a domestic violence advocate who gives women hope through her story. Everything works together for your benefit, but your words can help or hurt your path and those around you. Think of it this way: What good is the beautiful life (lifestyle) you've always imagined without a testimony to keep you humble and to encourage others who may go through similar trials. If you do not actively practice positive affirmations, the negative things that go through your head and come out of your mouth will eventually affirm your life.

WHERE THE MIND GOES THE MOUTH FOLLOWS

Where do you allow your thoughts about yourself and others to rest? Where do these thoughts lead you? What you believe about yourself is true, and what you believe about others is *your* truth. Keep in mind that as much as what you believe about others is *your* truth, so is what they believe about you. Knowing this, also consider how much harder it will be to change the perception of someone who is deadest on how they view you if you are deadest on how you see them.

To end negative self-talk, you must first be aware that it's happening. Anything that contradicts what you are working to accomplish more than likely goes into this category. How often do we kill our own dreams with our mouths? Every time we say, "I don't have this or that, so I can't do this or that," we release the results of those limitations. These words are just as powerful as positive affirmations and much easier to transform themselves into reality because when we believe them, we usually also lack effort. You are actively choosing which power source to feed by what comes out of you. To change the way you think, listen to your thoughts and pay attention to what you say. Rehash what you think before and after you speak. When you realize the consistency of how you think and what your words contribute or take away from you, you will have the ability to control those thoughts, and the choice will be yours to speak and create the story you desire for your life.

Write yourself a challenge statement affirmation: Ex: I challenge myself to remain optimistic, to speak life into myself and others, and to take action on the things I want to accomplish. Don't just write it and say it; feel it, break down each piece and meditate on it.

You can also simplify the challenge statement into an affirmation. Ex: I am optimistic, I speak life into myself and others, and I take action on the things I want to accomplish.

As if it were yesterday, I can remember sitting in a cubicle working and one person after the next would come by my desk to vent, gossip, or complain. I wondered why these conversations chose me, I was the last person who wanted to hear anyone talk about another person. I went as far as putting a sign on my wall that said, "No gossiping." That still didn't work. People would read it aloud and laugh as they proceeded with negative talk/gossip. Their *negative talk* caused me to have *negative self-talk* in my head about them. I share this so you can keep in mind how easily this can spread. There are many avenues that cause NST to become a part of our daily ritual, which is why we must be intentional in combating it. I spend time listening to positive messages, reading positive literature, and reciting affirmations as a way to counteract NST. The more positive fuel I put in me, the less room I have for things that work against me. What will you commit to doing to change the way you think? Spend some time considering where you take your thoughts.

At another time when you are not reading this book try sitting in a chair with your eyes closed. When the first thought enters your mind, consider how often you think about that. Is the thought something that contributes to your journey? Is it something inappropriate? Does this thought add value to you or anyone else in any way? After answering these questions, try this exercise again and this time intentionally impart the thought you want to replace your last thought with. This is the activity I use to meditate while actively working on my thought life. Don't be discouraged by thinking this takes too much effort, it's as simple as a daydream. Do it as often as you feel in an effort to change the way you operate when it comes to the cycle of thoughts- to words- to actions. You have total control over more things that have to do with your life than you think. What you entertain with your eyes and ears has everything to do with where your thoughts go, which is why it is important to monitor what goes into your ear and eye gates. The plainest version of this statement is to simply refer to children. They are far more pure before being put in front of a television or hearing adults curse. Like a wordless book being written as the author speaks, so is your life as you affirm it. Guard your gates. Negative self-talk limits your life.

SHINE

Use your words as weapons against negative inner chatter. When negative thoughts come into your mind, affirm yourself aloud by speaking the positive changes you wish to see take place, and believe what you say. Feel free to start with "I am..." I am beautiful, I am smart, I am loyal, I operate with integrity, I take care of my body, etc. Claim how you desire to see yourself verbally and with confidence.

AFFIRMATIONS

I am limitless. I have power over the outcome of my life. That power resides in my words. I align my words with my actions. I have a good life.

CHAPTER 5

Embrace Your Natural Gifts and Abilities

Natural gifts are areas that you put little effort into whereas others may have to work hard or practice to achieve the same results. From the ability to sing, draw, do math well, make people feel welcome and at ease, playing an instrument, making sense of things that seem hard for others, being an excellent cook, coming up with innovative ideas, being good with kids, having amazing wisdom, and so on are examples of natural gifts (when the fullness of them are more innate than taught). We all have natural gifts and talents whether we are aware of them or not.

It is often easier for others to recognize them in us because we typically operate from the mindset of what we want to do versus what's naturally in us. Do you know someone that if asked to decorate a room they leave it looking like a five-star hotel lobby but all they want to do is write crime novels? Some people don't use their gifts for many different reasons, but more of us would if we knew how they applied to our future and that those are the missing pieces that get us to the place we ultimately desire. Everything God gave us is meant to be used, and He gave us everything we need, read (2 Peter 1:3). But let us not be confused by the word "godliness" in this verse. When I hear "godliness," I hear God-like, meaning similar in power and ability. This is why it's important to read the Word of God for yourself and not to be spoon-fed what someone else receives. You may find things that speak to different situations in your life based on where you are right now from the same words someone else got something different from. The goal in embracing our natural gifts and abilities is to be open to what we have so that it may be effectively used and applied to who we become. Like a butterfly knows not of its caterpillar state, we too will evolve into a new place that requires the use of dormant abilities. The caterpillar is bound to the ground and can only fly after having used its natural ability to cocoon. What if it liked the feeling of the ground so much that it chose to stick with that? It would never know what flight looks like. Imagine the caterpillar envying the butterfly, not knowing that all it has to do is use its natural talents to become one. I learned an interesting fact in middle school that if you really thing about it, it's kind of amazing. No two butterflies are exactly alike. And just like people around you have their own gifts and abilities that may or may not be similar to yours, their timing is not yours and their butterfly (life) may not look like yours. The embracing of what you have and where you are going begins in your mind. It is okay to like who you are becoming and not let others dictate who that "new you" should be. Take criticism, rejection, ideas, and suggestions as something to consider, not a guide to your path.

If you have ideas about the things you are naturally good at, write them down. This may sound silly, but when we put things on paper, say them aloud, and act on them, they become reality. I remember when I was about fifteen years old, I sat on my aunt's couch and constantly rewound the tapes to all the songs I liked and wrote down the words. It was important for me to memorize those songs and I had no idea why. Shortly after, I began to write my own music and continued to do so for years. Now that I have written many mystery novels, I can tell anyone the entire stories from beginning to end without looking at them even though some of them are not completely written. On our journeys, sometimes we don't know why we are led to do things that will later benefit us. How does *this* benefit *me*? Because the reaction I get from sharing something I created with someone else is what reminds me of how gifted I am in that area. Memorizing those songs years ago has also helped my memory overall. I had a boss who would always say, "Well if Kurinn said I said it, I must have said it." This was his response after getting to know me, and seeing for himself how I could recall events based on triggered words. He couldn't promise us anything and not deliver without my co-workers bringing it up and saying, "Tell him Kurinn". My passion for writing has always been inside me like a necessary organ. Whether I wanted it or not, the circumference of this natural ability has many layers that fills in the blanks in other areas of my life. What enhancers are you neglecting by turning your back on things with which you have been gifted?

I wrote down all the things I knew how to do well and all of the things I wanted to do. Today as I reflect on my life and the gifts and talents I recognized at a young age, I can see all of my desires happening in some way, even if slightly different from how I imagined. I've always wanted to write; today I am a published author who writes multiple genres. I wanted to use my creativity; I do so through art. Building kids' self-esteem is important to me, so I work with youth through different organizations. I have a passion to help people with disabilities, so I spent my lunch breaks in middle school feeding handicapped kids, and have since worked with and/or spent time with children with autism and other organizations. I've always wanted to help people in general, but more specifically through words of encouragement or sound advice; I am a certified life coach. All of these things didn't happen at once, but as long as I dedicated parts of me to these areas in some way, I was able to achieve everything I wanted in these areas, and I'm not done yet.

I know at times it can be easy to put your gifts and talents to the side and seek other desires, but think of it this way: If you celebrated your birthday with friends and everyone brought you a gift, would you look at the boxes, leave them beautifully stacked and ask for another? How do you know what's inside each gift without unboxing and using them? This is what it's like to not embrace your natural gifts. You'll never know what resides in the circumference of one of them that may be the key that unlocks the door to your desires.

I told God years ago that my hands were open. I was tired of trying to figure out my life's path by controlling every aspect to make sure everything went according to my plan, based on what I thought I knew and the little I could see. It was as if He took my hands and pulled me in the right direction. With open hands, I was telling Him that He had permission to remove anything that did not belong to me and replace it with what He has for me. While many chase happiness, they have no clue that happiness is also chasing them, from the inside. With open hands, I actively took jobs that only paid me in experience. I did a lot of work for free and went through a long period of only having enough money to pay bills and put gas in my car to get to the next place. I turned down opportunities to receive things from people where I felt it might leave me owing or only using them to get where I saw myself going. It wasn't that I was prideful; it was more so me using discernment to keep a clean slate and to look beyond my current moment of need. Sometimes when we make decisions in the heat of the moment, we put ourselves in a position to be at the mercy of someone else without having thought things through. Yes, we need people, but we must also realize that we have in us everything we need to be who we were meant to be, including discernment. We have to make smart choices.

The things I gave up or let go of freed me from being stagnant, leaving me with piece of mind and allowing the Universe to work on my behalf. Opening your hands means operating differently. In no way am I saying to work for free or take every opportunity that comes along, or even to turn down help. I am saying be open to changing your perspective by thoughtfully considering everything that's at stake. If you want different results you must act out of a different nature. Your natural gifts and talents will lead you. If you are wondering what your natural gifts are, spend some time alone and think about what you are complimented on the most. What do you love about yourself? What could you do with your eyes closed because it takes that little effort? Because some of us aren't sharing or using our gifts, there are unmet needs all over the world. Like a job with many positions to be filled, when people see what you have to offer, you will then be placed. Not necessarily placed as in put to work, but more so positioned for your purpose. Even if you're operating within a gift you have no passion for, you will still encounter people who have access to the avenue you desire through your obedience to embrace what you were gifted.

SHINE

Once you begin to tap into who you were created to be, doors will fly open in many areas of your life. I am telling you firsthand that once I became completely open to whatever the Universe had for me, things I have wanted for years came to me effortlessly. My hard work in one area paid off in another. Everything I asked for was given, but it wasn't until I first used the gifts and talents I was born with. I never knew these things had the power to release my burning desires. What's for you will always be for you. Even if you waste time by putting it on the back burner, it will still be yours.

AFFIRMATION

I am gifted in areas only I can fulfill the purpose of being here for.

CHAPTER 6

Identify Your Weaknesses

After having completed the exercises in Chapter one and spending some alone time, you should be more aware of some of your weaknesses. Even if those weaknesses are in your thoughts, the best thing you can do for yourself is to address them. Active weaknesses can be dangerous. Why? Because what is active thrives, and anything that thrives develops vigorously. If you work out, you know that over time you will build muscle or become lean because your body is actively thriving as a result of what you allow to take place within it. So is the same for any active weakness. It is imperative that you perform your own self-check and write down what you find. Only you know your thoughts, motives, and true intentions unless your actions blatantly align, causing others to see them also.

Externally and internally, take a look at the things you are aware of and have control of, such as the way you dress, how you respond to others in moments of conflict, how you communicate, if you are judgmental at the sight of others (i.e., feeling compelled to verbally address their physical appearance), and pay close attention to the things that prevent you from getting opportunities. Some of these things can be a reflection of an internal lack, others a result of unawareness or contentment with the way you are.

Internal lack is being used here to refer to one who may have low self-esteem. How we see ourselves directly affects how we respond to everything around us. Low self-esteem works in several ways. It can cause one to be overly conscious of everything about themselves and create a lack of confidence, or it can cause one to be critical and analyze others. It's hard to shine when your mind is cluttered with judgment (be it on yourself or others). The easiest way to stop judging is to first realize that this is a negative affirmation and to understand that it brings no value to your life whatsoever.

Unawareness can be tricky because it's hard to address something you have no knowledge of. One thing you can do for certain is to think about what you think about. When communicating with others, try replaying in your mind what you've said or done to them. Role reversal, even when done alone, is an excellent tool to identify what you are putting out. Ask yourself, *If someone said to me what I said to them would I like it or not?* I actually dealt with this a lot in a previous relationship. There were many things said to me that clearly proved the other person either didn't care what came out of their mouth or they were unaware of the affect their words had. I asked a few times, "If I said (repeated statement) to you, how would you feel or respond?" The answer was consistently the same. "I would not like for someone to say that to me." The same goes for actions; ask yourself if someone else acted the same way you did in a certain circumstance, would it be okay with you. As simple as this exercise sounds, many never think to do it. And as easy as it is, it quickly builds awareness. This exercise is one that will prevent you from having to have your weaknesses constantly pointed out. It will be helpful if you take the conscious step to think things through and truly practice (Luke 6:31).

Is contentment wrong? It is when it negatively affects yourself or others. There is nothing wrong with being content in stable areas of your life but in areas of weakness, if you're okay with it, try not to force your position on others. For example, if you are okay being known as the one who's always late, you cannot expect other people to accommodate your shortcomings. One of my pet peeves in the past was when I would plan a birthday dinner and people would arrive late. I would tell them the arrival time was a half hour earlier so we could spend that time chatting, giving everyone time to get there, and so we could get seated on time. Unfortunately, there were times when people still showed up an additional half hour late. This was a big deal for me because my ego was set on my "me day." I am the birthday girl and I shouldn't have to wait for my entire party to show up before I am seated. How rude! This is an example of how what we become content with about ourselves affects others. My table could have been given away because reservations expire after fifteen to thirty minutes, I may have not eaten for hours with hopes of eating at the time I scheduled the dinner for, or someone might've had to leave after an hour of waiting and not get a chance to have dinner at all, and so on. Think about the things you may have become content with that aren't necessarily the end of the world, but they also aren't positive. Would you like them to happen to you? This will help you to see your actions from the perspective of others, and to work toward representing someone who cares about other people's time. What we are known for is written on the visual resume of our reputation.

When it comes to missed opportunities, is this a result of procrastination, unpreparedness, a lackadaisical attitude towards life, a lack of knowledge, or more? The next time someone else receives an opportunity that you believe should have been yours, observe your response to it. Do you lash out on their character, trying to find a way to justify why they didn't deserve it? Are you defensive? Do you tell yourself you didn't want it in the first place? Or do you sit down and analyze your role and what you brought to the table. When we reach the place where we can look at ourselves and then prepare for the next opportunity, versus blaming someone else whether right or wrong, that's where true growth begins.

Shining is a character attribute that speaks for itself. I am not telling you to beat yourself up when things don't go your way, I am asking you to build yourself up to activate the counteractive combats for your weaknesses. Just like a battery has a positive and a negative, and just as opposites attract, buried within every weakness is a strength. Whether you are weak at managing your finances, being promiscuous, eating too much bread, etc.—there is something inside of you made to win against it. But this is an area in life where you have to be intentional. We can combat weaknesses by first becoming aware of them and then by actively addressing them. If you are aware but continue to respond the same, nothing will change. You must make a conscious effort to pull from your strong points to defeat your weaknesses. Although they may not diminish completely, changing your habits can eliminate their strength, causing them to be far and few between rather than what you are known for. Identify your weaknesses and slay them.

SHINE

Everyone has weaknesses. The key is to not rest in them, allowing them to take root and become the core of who you are. Relax in your areas of strength, knowing that you were created for much greater. Show life who you are by living on purpose every day, and show yourself you have the power to control what you do by the actions you choose to take.

AFFIRMATIONS

Even my weaknesses work on my behalf. I am stronger than my strongest weakness. I overcome weaknesses through awareness and action. Active faith slays my weaknesses.

CHAPTER 7

Never Give Up

Throwing your hands up when it comes to giving yourself the opportunity to be the best *you* is equivalent to lying in a casket to sleep every night when you own a beautiful, plush bed. You're not preparing for death, so get out of that casket. Life can seem hard when you don't see results, but the results have no choice but to show up when you are persistent. My faith was tested in every area I could imagine throughout different stages of my life, but in the areas where I kept going is where the miracles happened. We are all just around the corner from our desires; the problem is that we give up or change course only feet away from the breakthroughs and have no idea. When I worked a 9-5, I knew what my finances would look like every two weeks. No matter what took place, I knew I would get paid on the 1st and the 15th of every month. By choosing to become an entrepreneur, I gave up the right to know my financial forecasts. I am now the boss and the staff. I am responsible for the success and failures that may come, but I am also limitless, and that is what I choose to gravitate to on my journey. Choose to lean toward the ideals that align with what you want. For me, the experience of not being able to know how I would take care of myself provided the challenge and ability to trust God even more.

We all have the power to achieve whatever we want as long as we're willing to work for it. This goes for every area of all of our lives. What stops many from achieving greatness within is the antagonistic tools of the enemy, which causes "the give-up." The enemy knows that if you saw even a glimpse of the godliness you possess, your faith alone would cause his mediocre power to just die. And if you are a believer, the enemy wants you to doubt your birthright because he is fully aware of what you are really capable of. His only job is to distract you (steal, kill, destroy- John 10:10), so of course he will do his best to invade your mind so you never reach your potential. But one thing about the enemy that is certain is that his power does not measure up to yours. Knowing this provides you the weapons you need to defeat him, but in order to win you have to keep going.

Choose what your "keep going" foundation will be built on and stick with it. Will it be integrity, tenacity, hope, faith? Whatever you choose, do your best to steer clear from choosing things like spitefulness, the "I'll show them" attitude, the desire to boast, or revenge. The foundation of your "WHY" can be used to propel you or else to stunt your movement. Choose wisely and show up for yourself every chance you get. This is important because what dwells inside you shapes the results of what you end up with. Think of this the same as you would the core of a light bulb. Just like us, there are positives and negatives inside that work together to perform a miracle: light. What resides in the core of an LED bulb is different from what's inside an incandescent bulb, and that difference causes the LED bulb to last 50,000 hours over the 1,200 hours the incandescent bulb has the ability to shine. If you are doing what you're doing for the wrong reasons in your heart, you still have a chance to change them now. Life provides more choices than we can fathom. Always choose what aligns with where you see yourself going and remember that getting there is only a part of the successes you aim for. Sustainability is the bigger goal. And just like these two light bulbs have different cores, so do you and the person you compete with or compare yourself to. You may appear to be the same, but you are not the same. You were built for a specific purpose and so were they. Focus on yourself and your lane.

GIVING UP ON PEOPLE...GIVING UP ON YOUR CHARACTER

When people disappoint us or do things we find to be offensive, there's no reason to throw them away. We all make mistakes, and forgiveness exists so we can live with clear hearts and minds. My goal when it comes to people I encounter is to figure out what role they play in my path, whether from a growth standpoint if challenging, or from a love standpoint in experiences, etc.

Years ago, I was presented with an amazing opportunity and I needed a service from a particular industry. I had reservations about using the person who I had used several times before because of a bad experience (the last of the person's work was of poor quality), but I presented the opportunity anyway. In lieu of having offered the person the job, something that would open doors for this person that surpassed where they were professionally, I asked God to reveal to me if this person is the one I should go with. All kinds of havoc broke lose. I remember having two thoughts go through my head as she showed herself unworthy. *I can't believe this is happening,* and *wow, I asked God to show me, and here it is, an unpleasant and unexpected blow-up.* (Listen to your instincts.) Sometimes we want to give people a chance because we believe in them/their gifts, even when they disprove themselves, but everyone is not meant to be attached to your destiny. Accepting this means understanding that you have reached the fork in your paths and they cannot continue the journey with you. I could tell that her outburst and further actions made her believe she won something, but when it comes to being at odds in any relationship, when you win, you lose. If there's anything to win, it is the ability to strengthen your character. In hindsight, when I reassessed the situation, I won that day. I could have called her out on her poor work and made her feel bad; I could have allowed her actions to provoke me, causing me to come down to a level I mastered conquering long ago, or I could have cut her so deep with words that she'd cry. As undeserving as I felt she was, I couldn't understand how we got to such a negative place when I had only been kind to her. I won because I lost the battle but gained even more integrity for not allowing her to activate the worst in me. I realized how much I had at stake and that being mediocre cannot be a character flaw that follows me unless I actively choose to limit myself.

Always consider what you have to lose when dealing with difficult people. Most times, people who act out negatively have nothing to lose and will take you down if you're willing to roll in the mud with them. Think about situations in which you've given away your "next level" by becoming a turtle when you were born to be a giraffe. T.D Jakes taught a message where he spoke about the giraffe that eats from the top of the trees and the turtle that eats its remnants from the ground. In so many words, he said, the turtle began to taunt the giraffe, but it would be unnatural for the giraffe to break its neck or suffer any discomfort to stoop to a level beneath its natural creation. This does not mean to demean another person, or believe you are above another for any reason. Here, the giraffe and the turtle represent behaviors. Although the giraffe does bend its neck for water and other necessities, it does not allow distractions that are only there to destroy its purpose. None of this diminishes the turtle's value; the point here is positioning. Understand *your* position and place the turtles in your life in *its* rightful position and operate with it from within that space.

Just because a person is not meant for you in one vein, doesn't mean he or she did not have valid purpose in your life. Throwing our hands up and walking away is what we're more familiar with as giving up, but allowing someone to take us out of character is even worse. This stains our reputation, fails our self-control, and robs opportunities. You have to learn how to respond to the things or people who have been given the assignment to stop you from reaching your full potential. There is enough pressure in doing what needs to be done to get to where you are trying to go without having to surrender to things that will only hinder you from getting there. Remember the reasons that you endure along the way; this will help you to maximize your ability to completely shine. What takes long hours, missed meals, tears, gas money, time, and effort to build can be lost in a moment, is it worth the 'give-up'?

If you're at a place where you feel that you've done all you can, you see no results, and you think what you're doing is useless or not meant to be, I am here to tell you that if it's in you, you can do it. Coaches, counselors, therapists, teachers, mentors, and many other resources exist to help you achieve your goals. Use them. When seeking any of the above, make sure they specialize in the area in which you need help. If you work with your hands, seek a mentor who has experience with his or her hands. You may find someone who is unofficially titled but can still help you. If you are seeking someone who is certified, ask him or her before you begin the process. The most important step is to take action.

REPOSITIONING:
KNOW WHO'S RIDING FOR YOU

One of the hardest pills to swallow is when you begin to walk in your purpose and people who have been in your life for years fall to the wayside. When I became an entrepreneur my friend circle changed without me taking any active steps to change it. I used to wonder why I didn't get any support from people who were once close to me. It was upsetting because I needed them, or at least I thought I did. I didn't realize how lonely and challenging the road of entrepreneurship was until the foundation of my career began to take shape. The stronger my foundation became, the number of people around me decreased. The strange part about this is that two people I thought would be with me in some way on my journey were actually supporting me from a place of responding positively to the marketing I was putting out until they found out it was me. The support stopped almost immediately. The one I had been closest to never asked me one question about how business was going, if I needed help with anything, and never brought up anything about my business in any conversations. Others distanced themselves, and I couldn't figure out why. I came to realize that what you have in common with people tends to drive where you go with them. Can they not take being in the presence of someone so fearless, even though I struggled for a long time to get my footing? Were they intimidated by what they saw happening in my life, not knowing how hard it was for me to wake up every day and give my all to something that was reaping no results and could have failed? Did it make them feel uncomfortable because they too had dreams that they just weren't ready to fulfill and I was actively doing so? None of that matters. We can still be friends, but they have repositioned themselves. Those who remained genuine were meant to be with me and they are the ones who will benefit from the growth of the seeds I've planted.

Look at your life from the standpoint of not condemning people who spare you from having to cut them off for one reason or another. Focusing on who left or distanced themselves is useless energy that can be given to those who are with you now.

LACK OF RESULTS RIGHT NOW DO NOT EQUATE TO A WASTE OF TIME

Just because you don't see results does not mean they aren't on their way. Think about this from the perspective of a bamboo tree. Planting any seed is equivalent to the foundation you are building in any area, from relationships to building a business and so on. When a bamboo tree is planted, there will be no activity above ground for three years, but in that third year the bamboo will surface and rapidly grow as high as thirty feet depending on its type (www.bamboogarden.com). Wherever you are right now in the process of what you've started or what you're building, you won't always see results right away, but no effort is wasted. When you give up on the seeds you plant, it doesn't mean they stop growing; it simply means you've turned your back on the fruit someone else will eat. How many seemingly abandoned apple trees have you come across where all you have to do is pick an apple, walk away, and eat it? Unclaimed fruit will always be consumed by someone or something.

Have you ever applied for a promotion, different position, or an increase in pay but none of those things panned out. It's time for a self-check. There is no reason to give up on these things; however, there is every reason to be open to what you discover about yourself and the root reasons as to why you did not excel in these areas. Are you aiming for these things out of genuine desire or because someone is challenging you to do so? This is a question you must be honest with yourself about. When things are placed in our hearts it's usually because we are being led to them, but when we act out of someone else's desire (lane), we are not adhering to our path. If this is a genuine desire and nothing seems to be in your favor, assess whether or not you are qualified for what you are aiming for. If not, qualify yourself in all areas (education or abilities/skills/wardrobe/timeliness, etc.) and proceed. Is this job where you are supposed to be, or is your promotion at a different place of business, or perhaps are you meant to be an entrepreneur? The root of your goals is just as important as the work you put in and the challenges you face that are meant to lead you down the right path. Refer to Joseph in the book of Genesis. He maintained his integrity and faith through a series of unfortunate circumstances that should have caused him to give up. His "WHY" was the vision he received from his dream. He faced many challenges before finally seeing his vision come alive—from being thrown into a well by his brothers (with whom he shared his dream), to being sold into slavery by the same brothers, to being thrown into prison for a crime he didn't commit, but using his gifts and talents along the way to gain the recognition and respect of Pharaoh, a king who later made him the ruler of Egypt.

This same assessment and endurance is required for our goals and in our relationships with people. Are you truly meant to be exactly where you are right now? If you believe you are, work on your communication and actions, and if not, make sound decisions, and choose your future paths without hurting anyone. Honesty is something people with integrity do not fear because they usually live a lifestyle that they don't have to apologize for. If you're not yet someone living this way, practice. This makes it easier for you to say what you have to say to others without hurting them as much as a lie would. This requires a level of maturity that comes from a place of thoughtfulness.

SHINE

If you want to see something thrive, feed it with love, be it your dreams, relationships, goals, or passions. If you love yourself first and then pour that love into your abilities, your shine will radiate with very little effort. The direct path to your breakthrough, miracles, and extraordinary blessings is the ability to keep going. Never give up on yourself, your dreams, your character, or people. If you keep going, your dreams will come alive, but your character is a necessary tool to get the best position possible within your vision. And because God meets us where we are, we have to learn to do the same with people. Long-handle spoons were made for a reason, everyone doesn't have to be close to us, but let's not feed friends or enemies with a dirty one. Cutting people off isn't a bad thing; it's how we do it that causes negative energy to follow us. Keep your path as clear as possible so that nothing prevents you from living your dream.

AFFIRMATIONS

Giving up on myself is not an option; my dreams are alive and thriving. Whenever I keep going, the results blow me away.

I don't give up on people; I reposition them and lift them up in prayer. When they reposition themselves, I accept the reason for them entering my life as <u>enough</u> and let them go. Those who have left me have taught me the value in those who are with me. I invest in them.

CHAPTER 8

Yearn to Be Yourself and No One Else

Imagine a long hallway with multiple doors on each side. There's a small glass window at the top of each door and a nameplate beneath the window. Although you see the names and recognize the path to your own door, curiosity, jealousy, mind changes, or the idea that you can do it better draws you to someone else's path, causing you to want to see more. Don't be distracted by what is designated for someone else. Stay focused on your course. This is how years pass before you reach your destination, even though you have a key to the door that is lit up and clearly marked for you.

It all starts with a peek into someone else's life, and then your thoughts begin to drift with you creating a plan to outshine them in something that simply wasn't meant for you. If you only knew what awaited you, you would have tunnel vision as you walk down that hallway. It is okay to admire someone, even if in secret. It is also okay to want to be like them in areas they seem to shine in without trying. What is not okay is plugging your power cord into their socket. Feeding off of the energy of others only satisfies for a moment because outside of their presence, you will still be you and they will still be them. The things that took place in their past to shape their life are not the same as the things that took place in your past to shape yours. Even though your paths may be similar, and even if you grew up in the same household, your destinations are not the same. Failure to understand this prevents many people from shining in their lane. Focus on the path to your door with the confidence that once you get there you will have wished you didn't waste your time trying to be like someone whose ultimate goals are not the same as yours.

Have you ever wondered why a person you may have encountered attracts certain people without even trying? Or why they seem to always have good ideas? They are more than likely using their key and spending time behind their own door. Have you tried to mimic what you believe you saw in them to get the same reaction or outcome for yourself? Sometimes it works and sometimes it doesn't, right? But those times it works makes you believe that this is the way to the top for you. By not tapping into your inner self you will always vie for something you already have. Limiting yourself by mimicking what you think is great in others is not your maximum capacity. In the end, all you are doing is proving that you can imitate another person, but why go through the process of finding out who you are if not to wholly be that person? If you knew what you possessed, being anything less would offend you. Imagine the best results your mind can fathom about yourself. Now accept that your designated shine is even brighter than that.

When you see the attention or reaction someone else gets by simply being themselves, remember that you too have something to offer that just may be different, and may fulfill another desire people have that was not fulfilled by what you saw in someone else. Every time you settle for imitating someone, you rob the people around you from a genuine experience and from getting something that could add value to their life. What if your destination required 100% of you, but because you choose to act in someone else's character or step into their lane, you only give yourself 88%. What if there was something about you that could get you everything you wanted, but by you acting as someone else, you only got their results? It may appear to be good, but what if being yourself could actually open a bigger door? Don't shortchange yourself by lowering your standards, assuming anyone is better than you or has more to offer than you. Salt is the most extreme seasoning because even one grain of it is as full of flavor as a many, but if it goes flat, it us useless. Don't lose the essence of your salt by trying to be like pepper.

The *lie* is that you don't have what it takes to get what you want out of life. If you've never fully been yourself, how do you know you want to be anything different? Many of us have had an "aha" moment after spending a substantial amount of time alone. We realize who we are and how attracted we are to the person we were born to be. Some have yet to have that moment, but it's not too late. Ask yourself, *what it is that I admire about this or that person?* Then ask yourself if you have fully explored who *you* are. Without comparing yourself to anyone, jot down the qualities you know you have, then meditate on these words:

No one has the ability to be me. My gifts are uniquely shaped for who I am. What I have to offer makes a distinctive difference in the world.

The more time you spend honing in on yourself, the less time you will have to vie for what someone else possesses. What are the makings of a great team? Someone has to fill every role in order for the team to win. In basketball, if the court was full of point guards, then who would shoot the ball? Differences are necessary to fulfill not only our individual purpose but also the bigger picture that connects us. My purpose is tied to yours, yours is tied to someone else's, and so on. I can neither fulfill my own or the bigger picture if I'm trying to be something that I am not. Don't allow what you perceive to be a distraction to detour you from what is meant for you. The desire to be or be like someone else leaves a void in the world that only *being you* can fill.

SHINE

If it didn't come from your core, your shine will be as bright as a flicker and won't have the ability to withstand such a glow as the sun. This does not mean no one can give ideas or suggestions to help you get to that place of maximum glow, but it does mean that if you copy or steal it, it will not have maximum power. A copy will never be as good as the original. The original of anything is always valued more. Find what makes you original. Spend some time focusing on yourself. Without the influence of anyone else, take the list of things you wrote about what you envy in others and see the difference in what you have to offer? What makes *you* attractive to people? What makes you stand out? What makes you different? When you find *your* space, *your* center, *your* sweet spot, no one can compete with it. Ground yourself in that space and allow your roots to go as deep as they possibly can. Nurture who you are by doing your best in the "I like me" areas.

AFFIRMATIONS

I know who I am.

I like who I am.

I am my biggest competition.

I have more to offer than I can imagine, and I desire to be my whole self.

I am wonderful.

CHAPTER 9

Overcome Barriers

We all have challenges and we all face barriers, but the key is knowing how to overcome them. If that key came in the form of a word it would be "energy."

Our reality is shaped by our beliefs, what we think of ourselves and others, how we view our abilities, and what we've been conditioned to expect from our past experiences. If you tell yourself every day that you attract positive people and experiences everywhere you go and you believe this in spite of what you see, you are right. You will attract exactly that! Energy is real; words have power and you are in control of what happens with yours moment by moment. Focus on how you respond to situations and think about what you can contribute positively. Your mindset should be dialed in on giving in proportion to what you expect to receive. If you want positive language around you, speak positively and surround yourself with people who do the same. If you want wealth around you, claim it and be wise with your income no matter how much or little you have. The same goes for relationships and possessions. Are you praying for a certain type of mate? If so, are you the person they would be attracted to? What if that person was standing right next to you but couldn't see you because you are not what he or she has been praying for? Are you a hoarder who can't let go of the possessions you already have but you still want more? Make space for what you want.

Some barriers are so evident and emotionally strong that we literally have no idea where to start to overcome them. Ask yourself what the root cause is for the barriers you currently face. Whether you've started a small business with no business plan or foundation, applied for a bank loan having poor credit, or just lost your job with upcoming mortgage payments—they all have a root cause that leads back to previous actions you've taken or the lack thereof. Instead of looking at where you are and preparing for a pity party, look back at what got you there in an effort to change the course of your future. Most of the barriers in our lives have one thing in common: us. How do we operate? One of the best things you can do at this point is to refer back to your life mission, vision, and values from the assessments in Chapter one. If you have not written them down, now would be a good time to do so. These components are just as important as a Fortune 500 company having a solid business foundation. You have to become the CEO in your life and operate based on the things you define as your core to eliminate the source of barriers you may be faced with. Your mission, vision, values, and belief system all work together in dictating what comes out of your mouth (your words can either give barriers strength or weaken them).

MINDSET MANAGEMENT

If you are someone gifted in baking, you probably don't need to follow a recipe to keep track of measurements. More than likely you use your eyes as a guide to know how much of each ingredient to include, and the taste is probably perfect. It's because you understand what you're making, what it should look like, how it should taste, and how many servings you'll get out of it. You may even be open to adding other ingredients that do not traditionally come in the dish. When we truly understand something it is easier for us to give room for change to take place which is necessary when faced with a situation that requires more than a one-note solution, following the same recipe (way of responding), time after time. What if you don't have all of the ingredients you need to complete the dish? Do you have what it takes to improvise? Not having an open mind, and operating as if what you know is all there is can be disastrous. The first step to overcoming barriers is to open your mind to new ideas, opinions, and ways of thinking. I am not telling you to be wide open to all things. I am telling you to claim discernment and wisdom daily in an effort to have the tools needed to figure out how to approach the barriers in your life. We all have people around us who have lived through different experiences. There stories are not just for our entertainment. The testimonies from others should be considered as free lessons. Listen to them intently to gain a perspective for how you would handle the same situation.

Secondly, use your words to write the future chapters of your life. Words are the most powerful weapon you own. Tell the barrier what to do. Sure, some barriers may seem impossible to overcome such as health, finances, the ability to conceive due to unforeseen circumstances, dealing with troubled youth, or repeating the same cycle because of lack of faith that things can actually change. But the Bible says, "Seek and ye shall find." Apply that to your barriers. When telling them what to do you must also put action behind your words. Look for answers by doing research. See how others manage troubled youth, find someone who dealt with or teaches on financial issues, read about alternative methods to conceiving, and continue to verbally claim the results you want. This is an example of God meeting you where you are. You face a problem and seek answers while speaking (in the present) the results you want to see. Always prepare yourself for what you want. Are you someone who wants to move further in your career but you refuse to do the small things that will get you there because you don't see how they apply (even though you know they can benefit you in some way)? Each small step toward removing brick after brick of the barrier in your life will propel you to where you are supposed to be.

I know firsthand how it feels to work hard at something that seems to reap no reward. All of the work I've done in my past for free, the wear and tear on my car, the lack of recognition for helping others, the struggle to strike a match to ignite an increase in my finances, positioning myself as an unpaid intern for people while also running my own business, and only sleeping an average of five hours a night actually paid off. Since those times, none of these things have been an issue because whenever they crossed my mind I would open my mouth and redirect my energy. Out came the words I wanted to dictate the outcome of my life. Ideas came out of nowhere; people invited me on radio shows, to travel, to speak, to collaborate, and so on. I continued to work every day in spite of challenges in my environment, believing that the work of my hands would remove the barriers in front of me, and asking for what I wanted, claiming what I wanted and not settling until I saw the results of what I wanted. I claimed travel and began to plan by businesses around the freedom to travel four months before the opportunities began to materialize. I claimed the exact amount of pay I would receive to speak and the types of audiences I would speak in front of while writing the first draft of this book. I claimed what my health would be like while eating better and working out. If faith without works is dead, what good is believing something without moving toward it? When you're hungry do you not get food? When sick do you not take medicine or see a doctor? Then why believe that you will get a new car without speaking it and actively living a life that draws it to you. Mindset management is the biggest tool in overcoming barriers. Until I learned to see the potential for God in everything, my thoughts gravitated to what was happening to me instead of how much control I had over the outcome.

Energy applied is power in action, the same as faith with works. You have power sockets in your home, but your television will only work if it's plugged in. When I began coaching, my clients taught me how to get the best out of them in their most defeated state. Some people face barriers that require a "faith-lift." It's easy to tell someone to have faith, but everyone doesn't know how to apply it. When I was seventeen years old, I wrote music almost every day. I can remember getting into an argument with my older sister. We were moments away from fisticuffs, but whenever it came to fighting, we'd usually tend to spare each other. Yes, I've been in a few fights. Needless to say, I never wanted to hurt anyone, but definitely not my sisters. I can remember the flaring of my nostrils and balled-up fists as she stood there provoking me. I stared at her with that 'I'll mess you up' expression on my face, but she wouldn't back down. It took everything in me not to hit her, and I don't know where the strength to walk away came from, but I went into the living room, pulled out my notebook, and began to write. This was the first time I can recall redirecting negative energy and putting it into something positive. A few hours later she came into the living room and asked me what I was writing. It was so good that I was glad she asked because I wanted to share it with someone. She was so blown away that she called my younger sister in to hear it. The smile on her face whipped away any anger I felt toward her and I realized how much power resided in forgiveness. I also realized how important the challenges are that we face, and when we redirect our energy, we give life in areas that require more from us to get results we desire that we may not have been aware of. This is step three in overcoming barriers. *You* control your energy. What if we had fought? What good thing would have come from that? What are you dealing with right now that can be managed in a way to support you and add value? If you are uncomfortable at your job, are you applying for work elsewhere? Have you gone to a temp agency and hit the ground by networking with other people to see what's out there, or are you sitting in your cubicle complaining, hence fighting with your sister? If you need money, have you assessed your skills and abilities to determine what you can do as a hobby that can make you money? If you want a husband or wife, are you currently husband or wife material? Are you complaining about not having a mate or are you actively investing in becoming whole (mind, body, and spirit) to be in the position to attract the type of person you want? Put your energy to work. Be what you want. There is no barrier bigger than the one who was given dominion over all things on earth and that's you. You can't control other people, but you can control what you get based on what you put out. It may not always be easy to choose what you should do or how you should do it in the moment, but anything can be accomplished with practice. Start there, and if all else fails, get a coach.

SHINE

Have a serious conversation with your CEO (yourself) to determine what lies behind the challenges you face and take the necessary steps to change those behaviors with the mindset of illuminating the things that cause barriers. You have the ability to dictate the entire course of your life. Make different decisions to get different results. Start small and eventually you will see the miracle of change taking place in your life. It's time to break the routine of choices that reap the same undesirable results.

103

AFFIRMATIONS

I was created to overcome barriers as a part of my testimony. There is nothing I cannot accomplish when I redirect my energy.

I believe in my ability to find creative ways around the things that appear to stop me from moving forward.

My faith is active. I am unstoppable.

CHAPTER 10

Use What You Have

We all have abilities, everyone may not be aware of theirs, but that doesn't make them any less real. Have you ever shied away from something you're good at because you're uncomfortable tapping into that source? Like talents, you are naturally gifted in these areas as a backup to how you execute the things you are passionate about. We may not always pour 100% into what we have, but in order to live a lifestyle in which we naturally shine, more is required from us than what we would typically contribute to or invest in ourselves. Some people minimize what others maximize, and the only difference between the two is what they do with what they have access to. There are those who will use every drop of what is available to them, whereas others may only touch the surface. What do you have, and to what degree are you using it?

Because I have a background in higher education, I first chose education coaching while going through my certification process, but when I had conversations with my mentor, someone who'd been coaching for over twenty years, he helped me realize that even though education coaching was something I could do with my eyes closed, it wasn't my passion. I still assist this type of client under the "life coaching" umbrella; however, I chose author coaching as my secondary specialization because of my passion for writing. I am using one of my natural gifts (author coaching) while simultaneously working within my passion (life coaching). Do I have other gifts and talents? Am I passionate about other things? Yes, but when I look at my life in total, I have to ask myself which of these things align with where I see myself going? This is one of the most powerful questions you will have to ask yourself in every area of your life. The answer may take some time based on you having opened all of your gifts to see where and how they fit into your life. It is important to know this because our shine has the potential to ignite at its capacity when we are in our lane(s).

I mentioned in the intro that I am a self-taught artist. Although I am not actively creating art, I see it playing a major role in my future dealings with kids. You too have dormant things you know how to do that may need to be applied to your life at some point. Nothing we have is to be wasted but to be managed on our journey. It's like that dress or suit in your closet with the tag still on it. In the back of your mind you're excited for the day to come when you can wear it, and usually when that day comes you feel good about the fact that you had it in the first place.

Have you ever been in this situation: You realized that what you have to work with doesn't seem to produce, even after everything was set up for a return to come in the future, but you needed a *now-return* on your investment? Here is the solution to that lack: Keep working toward what you want by continuing to massage what you currently have in your possession. Doing so will propel you in the direction that forces fruit to appear. Wake up each day affirming the same things, being thankful for them as if you already had them, while still encouraging other people. When you get frustrated use those emotions as fuel to continue working on every seed you've planted. Relationships may end, finances may lack, sometimes you may not get back what you deserved from people you gave to but you must take the next steps. If there came a time when I couldn't move forward because of money, that would be the point when I would pat myself on the back, knowing I had done all I could and the rest was up to God. When we continue to be faithful regardless of what should look like reality, He continues to honor us. People would often ask a close friend of mine, "How is Kurinn surviving?" I told her to tell them, "By the grace of God." They wanted a *real* answer, but nothing could be more real. We must turn our focus away from what we need and live in the moment of what we have. Honor what you ask for by committing to it and using what you have to get it. Doing so always produces more.

I've had people to tell me they don't know what they have, and some who know, don't know how to use it. A prime example of this is in 2 Kings Chapter four. The profit Elisha visited a widow that owed a debt to creditors who were coming to take her sons into slavery as payment. Elisha asked what she had in her house and she said, "Nothing but oil." He told her to borrow vessels, fill with oil, and sell them. She followed his instructions and paid her debt in full, leaving her and her sons with enough money to live off of. Sometimes we can't see what we have to work with but others can. In today's terms she became a successful entrepreneur. Prior to Elisha's instructions, the widow reminded him that her deceased husband had feared the Lord. When you are connected and actively exercising your faith, your Elisha will always come. Even when you are actively using what you have, your Elisha will still come. Mine has come many times to affirm my vision, keeping me on track. Using what you have requires looking at your life through different lenses. If you are someone in a place where you believe you don't know what you have or how to use it, start by waking up daily with a grateful attitude. Where we spend the most time in our thought life is where our lives gravitates to. Look at where you are right now. It traces back to your thoughts. Those thoughts lead to actions, and the energy you are putting out attracts all the things that surround those thoughts. Just like the woman with the oil, her thoughts were that she had nothing. She told the profit, "All I have is oil", minimizing what she should have been grateful for. What are you minimizing in your life that has the power to save you?

SHINE

You have something special. The world awaits your contribution as if a person sits on the edge of their seat in angst. Understand that what you have is connected to what someone else has and so on. Like a chain, many links are necessary for it to be so. Don't break the link; get in alignment by positioning yourself to be in place. Pray for discernment that you may recognize the Elisha's in your life. These messengers are like fuel for that burning flame inside you. Turning the air on in your home when it's 40 degrees outside is just as useless as applying energy to areas in your life that take away value. Connect the pieces that make the most sense. Be thoughtful about yourself and those around you. Give away what you don't need in an effort to make room for what you want. *You* may be someone else's Elisha in a different way. Maybe it's not by giving words but of things, and when you give, do it from a place of wanting to see them better off and not from a place of expecting something in return. Use everything you have to benefit yourself and others.

AFFIRMATIONS

I have everything I need to live the life I want now. I am in position to receive anything I believe I lack. I actively use what I have to get what I want.

CHAPTER 11

Recognize Your Lane

Isabella, a twelve-year-old girl, loves the way her mother dresses so much that she often tries on her clothes and models them in the mirror. One day she sneaks into the back of her mother's closet and tries on her wedding dress. Although the dress is beautiful, and fits her mother perfectly, Isabella realized she would have to grow into such a dress in order for it to compliment her physique. That was the last time she tried on her mother's clothes, but as she grew up, she adopted her mother's style.

Your time to receive the things you desire will come as you mature. Like Isabella's mother, other people may have grown into their success whereas to you it appears to be instant. Isabella has no idea what took place that caused her mother to choose each item in her closet. This is why Chapter eight is so important. If you don't understand a person's reasons or the events that led them to where they are, then do you really even know what you're copying? You may believe you want what they have because of what it looks like, but do you want their struggles too? To recognize your lane is to try on your own garments (use your gifts and talents) until you encounter the one that best fits who you are. It is better to know what your lane looks like before going down the wrong path, but sometimes the detour has to be the teacher. Just because I am a life coach does not mean that I look at other life coaches and do what I see them doing thinking that is *my* recipe for success. I may apply some general best practices, but regardless of what it looks like, I don't want their journey; I want all of what's mine and you should want all of what's yours.

Do you believe the reason you were born is to do exactly what someone else is doing, the same way they are doing it? If so, what makes you necessary? Let's not confuse this with the guise of things such as doctors. Of course you want everything about surgery, medicine and so on to be uniform. But who they are as individuals should not be a mirror lest they have nothing more to offer than a skill. There is something you have that is supposed to be discovered and shared with the world. When you shine in your lane, you serve the same purpose as a lighthouse. Your light serves as a navigational aid for someone else to reach their potential and to warn others of dangerous zones. The navigational aid is not for them to follow you; no one follows a lighthouse. The aid is for them to see where they are going in relation to where you are (your position). If you're in place, when your paths are aligned to cross, they can get from you what they need as they journey through their life. This could be in the form of advice, you being seen as an example, meeting your mate, getting promoted without applying, and so on. The danger zones are the reasons we need to see ourselves in the first place. What things about us have the ability to negatively affect the destination of others? There are people who have passed away and only then is their purpose highlighted for the rest of us to see.

CHANGING LANES

Be intentional about your self-discovery and don't be afraid to exhaust everything inside you to encounter it. Unbox each gift and use it. You have the right to change lanes as many times as it takes to find what it is that you are supposed to do. When in traffic, we change lanes all the time to get to our destination. The only difference then and now is that we usually know exactly where we're going when driving. Everything around us has the ability to either slow us down, cause an accident, or allow us to arrive on time. In life, the same applies. Who are you slowing down because you aren't using your gifts? What collision awaits because you are wasting time looking at what someone else is doing rather than focusing on the road (yourself)? Why wait until you've retired to start living within your gifts only to arrive at the idea that you're late? Understand that if you have breath in your body, it's not too late. Age is not a pre-requisite to SIYL. You're actually just in time. There has to be a mental readiness for us to be willing to shift from one gift to the next in search of the greatness we possess. Changing lanes requires patience with yourself, faith in your abilities, abandonment of fear, and the drive to take action. You have to be your biggest cheerleader with your eyes on the end goal and your mind set on the present moment of what it takes to get you there (envision where you want to be and act in accordance with getting there from where you are). Do your best not to be discouraged if you experience a lack of support around you. Sometimes when changing lanes, those who are closest to you can lose faith in you because you may appear to be a dream chaser. In these cases, it's better not to share every detail of what you're doing, or at least until you get to a place of clarity.

STAY IN YOUR LANE

We've all heard people say, "Stay in your lane," but how do you know what lane that is if you haven't discovered it? In the workplace, you know your role and should not step into other department roles trying to use what you have to shine. Be strategic and give your ideas to the manager over that department, leaving it up to him or her to decide if what you contributed is valuable for the team or the customers, and let it go. If you are antsy and feel the need to do this often, you may want to apply for a different position. If you are all over the place trying to shine in multiple departments to figure out your lane, you could end losing your job or being seen as an annoyance. Shining is an inside job that starts with an understanding that you can't force what you have on others. In the work environment, the big idea is to master what you are currently doing to shine at that. You are in a lane you chose; shine there and change lanes outside of work to discover your gifts and talents. As you discover them, apply them where you currently are. In the end, the light is not for you. It is supposed to be an attractive element that naturally glows and allows others to see what they should aim for within themselves. If you worked at a college in the career services department, would you walk around fixing computers because you've been self-taught and you're confident in your skills? What happens when you make a mistake is quite different than what happens to the IT staff if they do. When a part of a system, you must let the expert be the expert and focus on mastering your craft in an effort for the entire system to work properly. Do passengers on a plane try to fly it? Does the pilot serve drinks? Then neither should you step outside of your purpose as it relates to your assigned duties at work. Apply this same analogy to areas in your personal life. The changing of lanes specifically refers to your natural gifts and talents and can even be translated to our desires to try something new as long as it does not shift us out of order.

YOUR FIRST LOVE

If you're someone who struggles to find your lane, refer back to your first love. What did you want to do before money, time, or other people's successes fogged your vision? By going through the process of deep introspection, you will know what you are supposed to do simply because of the investment you're putting in yourself. The "HOW" will come as long as you are open to reaching your destination. Look at where you are right now and ask yourself if what you are doing with your life feels right? Are you living through people on TV? Are you at a job you dislike, waiting for the weekend week after week? Is there more you desire but you feel stuck and have no direction? What is that burning desire inside you that seems so far-fetched but you believe in it so much that it won't leave you?

Like Isabella in her mother's dress, each one of us has a specific S.H.A.P.E. that will determine the details of our lane. Spiritual gifts, Heart, Abilities, Personality, and Experiences (http://www.sbpcshape.org/).

This assessment will help you recognize your lane as far as direction. The active work that must take place within your lane is up to you. Have you ever studied for a test but once in class, you saw how the teacher favored Phillip so instead of you using what you had (tapping into what you studied, what you know) you settle for copying off of Phillip's test only to end up failing? We don't always see the details behind someone else's why which can lead us down the wrong path. In this case, the teacher saw that Phillip struggled and needed the extra attention. You have what it takes to be great, don't limit yourself by not recognizing that and settling for what someone else has. Know your S.H.A.P.E., and remember that of all the avenues you travel to find where you fit, you also have the ability to create our own lane.

PARTNERSHIPS

Here we are referring to all relationships where there is a commitment. Partnerships can be hard when both or all people have similar strengths. In some cases, each person may have his or her shine muffled by another unintentionally. This can cause the offended to fight for what he or she believes has been taken away to get back realigned with his or her familiar lane. In the case where these two or more individuals are in the same environment, one may notice the attention the other is getting and, realizing similar strengths in this area, this person oversteps a boundary by tightening a bulb when the room is already properly illuminated. What the person may fail to realize is that by focusing on what is seen versus focusing on self, the person is giving away efforts by displacing personal energy, and may be creating a wedge.

Let's say a couple visits their neighbors and the husband bakes a desert that has everyone crowded around him asking for the recipe. The wife knows she's a great cook and that her husband only knows how to bake this one dish. She's won prizes for her cooking and usually gets the attention he's getting, but she just can't take it. She butts in and makes it known that she too can bake and that she just won an award for the last recipe she created. She goes on and on. Why is it important for the wife to step into her husband's light, redirecting his shine? Clearly she's a good cook, but this is his moment. Your lane is where you naturally excel without added effort, not a place where you ever feel as though you must interrupt someone else's glow to be seen. Yes, baking may be her lane, but her actions have automatically dimmed her light. Why couldn't she bake for the next event and allow her and her husband to be seen as the couple that bakes fantastic deserts instead of *her* now being seen as the competitive wife? When we fail to recognize our place as something that cannot be taken from us, we can cause more harm to our own reputation than someone out to get us. Keep in mind that even when people don't say anything, you show them who you are by your actions. Sometimes to shine means to have confidence in your abilities specifically when the person next to you is being praised for what you may be able to do better. The execution is not as important as the humility you must possess to attract opportunities. Once you learn to accept how great you are in the presence of others who also glow, your character is strengthened. Your response to celebrate others highlights another quality that adds to your light. Think about this in terms of co-workers, business partners, and siblings. Pay attention to how you respond when others are being recognized and stop trying to fight for what is not at the time yours. If you feel intimidated, why not join forces to become a power team. A linebacker knows his role and does not switch places with a quarterback because the crowd went wild over his last play. If you want to know where you fit, refer back to your gifts and talents and sharpen your tools by focusing on you. Learn how to praise others without allowing jealously to intervene. The same way you need praise and affirming, so do others.

This is an important part of recognizing your lane. You can't stand in someone else's lane, tarnish their light, or extract their bulb and expect to shine. Even if it is as simple as a moment, anything you take *must* be replaced. You may not have control over those who steal from your light, but you can control what you take from or add to someone else's.

Narrow or wide, your lane is yours. When you see that someone else soars in multiple areas, try not to detour from your path. Imagine being lowered 500 feet from the air into a single space on the ground. If your eyes are on others the whole time how will you know what space you've been lowered into. Are you on the right path? When you can keep your eyes on you and what you should be doing, you will clearly see where you're going. Let go of the distraction of trying to see what someone else is doing. You can't move forward if you're constantly looking to your left or right. You are bound to bump into some unexpected roadblocks if you do. (Luke 19:42-44 NLT) says, *"How I wish today that you of all people would understand the way to peace. But now it is too late, and peace is hidden from your eyes. Before long your enemies will build ramparts against your walls and encircle you and close in on you from every side. They will crush you into the ground, and your children with you. Your enemies will not leave a single stone in place, because you did not recognize it when God visited you."* This is a powerful statement, but the first and last sentences are key. We have peace when we understand what's really important and what to focus on. The full story was referring to Jesus's arrival into Jerusalem and how the people responded by throwing their garments on the ground before him. There were naysayers who challenged their response, which caused Jesus to say these things to them. The naysayers are those who step into the lane of others to take the light off of them. Furthermore, the enemy is powerless when we recognize what God put in us. Focus on that.

SHINE

See yourself and recognize your strengths and weaknesses as you use your gifts and talents to shine in your lane. Allow any negative energies to be used as tools to push you into greatness. Try not to look at greatness as something far-fetched from you that only applies to those you see shining in their lane. You too are great; you just may not have accepted it yet. Where you are and what you have do not determine your greatness.

116

Your first breath into this world does. Simply by being alive, you give unlimited value that is constantly under attack. Always do, be, and give your best as you invest in yourself so that you may see where you are supposed to be. Once you recognize your lane, nothing can stop you from reaching your destination other than your lack of desire and actions to get there. Whether you see yourself as a leader or someone who provides amazing support, honor your position. If you are aiming at the wrong lane between the two, be honest with yourself about where you best fit based on execution and results. A supporter enhances a leader. Most leaders don't have the skills of a supporter so try not to allow the titles to dictate your level of greatness. They both need each other, and the fullness of one allows the other to shine.

AFFIRMATIONS

I believe I can have whatever I want, and if something is not meant for me, I am mature enough to accept it and remain open to what is mine. I recognize my lane.

CHAPTER 12

Learn Something New At Least Once a Week

Personal/professional development is essential for growth. Whatever we take in, we become full of. Just like babies drink milk for months but soon outgrow that phase and adapt the need for solid food, we too must make the necessary adjustments to accommodate the growth stages within us. What do you desire? Are you feeding yourself the proper things to accommodate such desires?

I often tell myself that information is the only degree between success and failure. The conception of this book derived from two places. One, my desire to help people discover what's in them. I've worked with clients who thought they couldn't achieve certain goals for countless reasons that really boiled down to time management and action. Even without certain resources, there are still pieces of the puzzle that can be put in place until those resources become available. The other reason was out of a place of frustration, dumbing myself down in certain settings to protect my inner voice. I remember thinking, *if I wrote a book, people would not only have access to an action driven, self-led coaching/consulting session, but I would also be able to leave a footprint in the earth that represents who I am, my coaching style, and what we really can achieve with a changed mind.* Take off the responsibility of placing others in a position that was created for you. You are responsible for showcasing the fullness of everything you possess. There is nothing new under the sun, but our minds are powerful enough to package a message that can reach the right people in a way they have never been reached before. This is why *your* voice is just as important as mine. The epiphany to write this book came long after I began affirming "Believe You Can Shine and You Will" as an outward affirmation to others, having no idea what it would lead to. This is the power of being open to what the Universe has for you, and being connected to your spirit. Being open allows us to give, and being connected allows us to receive. I considered mapping my specific self-development plan within these pages, but I realized by doing so that would only *limit* you. I'd rather challenge what you already know combined with your own research to see what you're made of rather than spoon-feed you my prescription. I've talked about how following someone else's method only allows you to go as far as they've gone. My hope for you is that you will go further, in the direction you're supposed to go. Although different things work for different people, you have to find the things that work for you and gradually add them to your daily routine.

The best way to learn something new daily is to create an outline that starts with the main thing. If the main thing is to become a top speaker, what qualities does a top speaker have? What kind of speaker are you trying to become? Will you be raw and uncut or corporate? Will you attend Toastmasters meetings or position yourself to lead and become the top speaker of those meetings? How will you dress? Does your personality match the answers to these questions? Where and who is your audience? Do you have a speaker sheet? What are your rates? Research can help you answer these questions. In this example, learning something new daily can be as simple as you looking for what states need speakers like you. Tomorrow, research what topics are lacking in your industry. The next day look into what qualities keep the audience's attention. And then find out how to collaborate with champions in different states that can help you find your target audience. This is all adding to the foundation of the one thing you want to do. Whether your goal is to be the next Top Speaker, Chef, Designer, Nanny, or HVAC provider etc., learn as much as you can about that one thing to dominate your lane. The more you seek, the more you will find what can lead to adding products to your service, or even adding an additional service to what you already offer. Once the door to development is open, your value has the potential to increase tremendously.

While developing your craft, *you* must also develop. Is using curse words acceptable for where you are going? If you are on the fence just ask yourself who you've seen that this works for and are you aiming for that type of light. What is required from you as an individual to get where you want to be? Does laziness, gossiping, tardiness, or radical behavior add value to your mission? If not, seek environments that challenge these things and force you to practice giving them up. Have you ever noticed how most people who have genuine success do not possess these qualities? And if they do, no one sees them (unless these qualities are specific to their industry). You can usually tell by what comes out of someone's mouth what's in his or her heart. The only way to minimize the things that take away from you is to spend more time in the things that add value to you. Sign up for a class, network with like-minded individuals, or get a mentor. Development should be a combination of enhancing your skills as well as your inner self. This is very important because one without the other leaves a gap in your movement.

While improving yourself, don't look down on anyone who is not doing what you are doing and try not to compare yourself to them or anyone else to justify why something is or isn't working them or for you.

You can't force people to accommodate your growth process by joining you on your journey, doing things the way you do, or changing their behaviors, but you can take control of directing your own journey by practicing the underlying principles in this book consistently.

Revisit your goals weekly to stay on track. Even if you have a ton of notes written here and there, keep one running log of all of your goals in every area you wish to be successful. They should be written in the form of an outline, which makes it easier to break down the main thing and to compartmentalize and set priorities. Seeing the progress allows you to celebrate the steps you've taken to get closer to what you want. I state my goals in the form of affirmations, claiming them daily to attract them to me, and believe it or not, it works. On your goals, add one simple thing that you can do to sharpen your mind in the direction you wish to enhance. Whether it's playing a sport or word game, learning to drive a different type of motor vehicle, reading a new book, watching a documentary, practicing a new skill, learning a different trade or language, or having a healthy debate on a choice topic—learning something new adds value.

Education is not a matter of only obtaining degrees; it is a matter of information and wisdom. There is no such thing as too much information when learning. Eventually you will have a mental catalog that will prepare you to go far beyond the limitation you've subconsciously placed on yourself. We all limit ourselves when we state why we can't get what we want. Positive affirmations counteract the word "can't." Having a list of daily affirmations is good, but actively stating them daily is great. Have you ever looked back at something you did in your past and now you see how it fit into your present day life (be it good or bad)? Every decision you make will play a role in your life. Invest just a little bit of time on things that could be considered above where you are and when you get to your destination you will see how these things applied to you having arrived at your goals.

SHINE

There will always be someone better at something than you, but there will never be another you. For this reason, when you shine, no one can compete with you. Increasing your knowledge is not spending money on another degree; the degree can be useless if you have no experience or lack interpersonal skills. Close the gap between where you're standing and where you desire to stand by volunteering, doing your own research, and applying what you've learned using your mentor's failures and successes as a navigational aid and tool to bypass dangerous areas. When you combine everything you have inside with these tools, you truly set yourself apart.

AFFIRMATIONS

I know what I know, but I can always know more.

I am full of knowledge and wisdom.

New ideas come to me in my sleep; I am a strategic genius.

CHAPTER 13

Aim Higher Than You Did Yesterday

Everything in this world is meant to be found. There is nothing hidden from us, so why do we limit ourselves with such self-slander. Aim higher than what you see, knowing that the lowest you could land is so far beyond your dreams that if you never made it higher, that place would suffice ten times over.

One of my favorite things to say to people is, "Whatever you *believe* is true." I believe someone's life will be changed in a positive way by reading these words. I also believe that decisions must be made now in order for you to see your vision unfold.

I was driving on the highway headed to my office on a Friday morning at 10 a.m. As I was driving I heard what sounded like a loud pop and a huge cloud of black smoke rose from the ground. At first I thought it was the exhaust from one of the Mack trucks in front of me, but the smoke kept coming. I was less than half a mile away from a plane that had fallen from the sky. Thick black smoke, fire, and a tire was all that was left. I thought it was a car until the news later revealed that it was a private plane that held three people and a dog. The close encounter I had with this fatal crash was enough reassurance that God still has a plan for me. The reality is that he has a plan for all of us (Jeremiah 29:11). Why does it take tragedy in someone else's life for us to see how precious life really is? Why is the wake-up call for us to chase our dreams buried within the remnants of death, hurt, and pain? We never know when our time will come, and rather than dwell on the what-ifs I challenge you to take action now. I still pray for the families and loved ones that crash impacted, and I often think about all the other people on the road that day and what they think about as it relates to their assignments in life. If you aim at nothing, where do you land? Nowhere. But if you aim at the most unattainable things that exist, what do you get? Farther than you were.

To aim higher than you did yesterday requires one thing: action. This word is what causes some of us to remain dreamers and others to do amazing things. The simplest conditions for this commitment are similar to someone who wants to get toned. They may have never worked out before but the act of doing five pushups today and six tomorrow and seven the next day until their body can withstand a set of 50 is what this looks like in any area we want to shine in. Do what you can and add to it every single day. Whether it's more research, making more calls, or perfecting your make-up. The idea is not to seek more and more and not being satisfied. The goal is to work that muscle until you clearly own the position you desire. Look at top performers like Prince. With every performance, his audience increased and his fan base grew far beyond where he started because his performance and music was just that good. How are you performing in your lane? Are you aiming high, or are you content where you are? Aiming higher than you did yesterday means whatever you do, don't decrease; you must either maintain with the efforts of becoming "the one" or compete with your last performance to outshine yourself. No one could out-perform Prince because he dominated his lane. That doesn't mean there aren't other great artists out there, because there are. However, he created something untouchable by making it his own and consistently outdoing himself; he remained his only competition.

SHINE

When you realize that no one can compete with the core of who you are, aiming higher becomes a natural element that propels you into your destiny. You have the power to leave the footprint behind that speaks on your behalf long after you're gone. Stretch your arms to the sky and give everything that holds you back to God. Remain open to action. Only you can limit where you land in life. Do not allow the perceived end to stop you from achieving your best life now, and don't be led to greater things by the demise of others. Channel your energy toward the movement you know is required from you to live the way you want from this very moment on. Nothing can stop you but you. We don't know when our time will end, but it is better to be living than dreaming when that time comes.

AFFIRMATIONS

The higher I aim, the closer I get to my dreams faster.

The sun and the moon are my guide to the next level; I am my biggest competition.

Everything I want is at my fingertips; my hands remain lifted to the sky.

CHAPTER 14

Nurture the Positive Seeds of Change in You

Feed the need to succeed no matter what. Now that you are guarding your ears and eyes and are openly active with personal/professional development, it's time to fuel your abilities. To do this, you will have to intentionally focus on the things you've learned until they become a part of who you are. Growth doesn't happen unless you are being stretched. The pain of growth always produces something that takes you from a state of good to better. Take an apple tree for example. When the apple buds there is a level of excitement because, even at its smallest, the sight of the budding apple is proof that the tree is alive and working according to what it was created to produce. Even though there's a level of excitement, it's better to pick the apple when it has finished growing to get the best results. During this process the coloring will change, the taste will change, and it may even fall off of the branch rather than someone having to pick it. There's no need to rush your growth process rather than apply these principles to allow a full process to take place.

Although the apple tree was planted with one seed that now has many branches and produces countless apples, they each grow at their own pace. This represents the many gifts and talents you have. You will have to learn how to shift your focus from one apple to the next as they bloom. What will it take for you to grow to the point of releasing yourself from the branch like the apple? Consistency. Feed each area in your life what it needs when necessary and eventually the full-bloomed tree will catch the attention of the right people.

SEASONS

Whenever we journey into our purpose, it is important that we not expect to see your growth in others. The most we can do for them is to be a support system and a lighthouse, not a domineering dictator.

By default your growth causes people to change. Some will desire to do and be better simply by watching you, and some will save you the heartache of having to cut them off by doing so themselves. You will have to learn how to see the potential for something good in every situation and not fault people or yourself for the severance of ties. Just like seasons change so too will people's positions in your life. Make certain that within your growth you are not doing something to cause people to distance themselves from you or it isn't growth that's happening; it may be judgment or some other difficulty. Know that as you get closer to your fully developed self in the journey of becoming who you were meant to be, you will be faced with challenges. Take them as lessons, experience, and tests that you will overcome as long as you don't give up. For those who want to leave, let them, and for those who want to stay, let them, as long as they are not hindering your growth.

For every positive habit you pick up, you must give it attention. Just like trees need rain and the sun, your positive seeds of change need to be nourished as well. Once you get into the habit of saying affirmations to yourself, write them down. Study them and add to them as they evolve. The same thing goes for working out if you choose to. Buy some gym clothes and create a steady routine to keep you going. All that is birthed from your growth will require consistent attention in an effort not to fade.

If you want to be a leader, do the things that meet the expectations of a leader so that it only makes since for you to be put in that position.

(There is nothing beyond your reach.) If I told you that everyone you have ever come into contact with has purpose in your life would you believe it? They do. The length of time doesn't matter; there is always something to learn even in an instant. Think about divine connections that take you back to what you needed when you met someone. If you hadn't messed up your favorite shirt, you wouldn't have ended up at the cleaners where you met a man who told you about a conference looking for speakers to travel to Europe but the deadline to sign up was two days away. Every person we meet in every place we go has a purpose in our lives no matter how big or small. We have to learn to be open and sensitive enough to realize it. How many times have you had a need that you prayed for and you wondered if it would ever be met, but in one instance you spoke to a stranger only to find out that person could meet that need? Are you someone who speaks to people you don't know in public? Why not? Try saying hi to a stranger with no expectations (recommended for adults). This opens doors.

SHINE

If you've ever planted a garden or even witnessed the growth of vegetation, you have seen the results of nurturing change. There first was dirt and all it took was the planting of a seed, water, and the sun before a miracle came out of the earth. If this is possible for something as minimal as a seed, what do you think would happen if you nurtured the things in you that also have the power to grow and become mind-blowing experiences?

AFFIRMATIONS

Everything I need is within me. I feed my core and my core produces results for me.

CHAPTER 15

Establish Yourself as the Expert

When we make decisions that turn out in our favor we give credit to what got us there, but with the same efforts, if things turn out opposite of what we desire, we tend to lose faith in our ability in that area. Look at your ability to complete something as a success regardless of the outcome. Not finishing what you start will always leave an unknowing, but completing anything you start is where real masters are born. To complete something fully, whether it works or not, allows you to become a resource for those in need of the knowledge from your experiences.

Do something different. You can't become an expert at something without having moved past that which holds you back. It would be like an English teacher completing a math problem the same way over and over again and never getting the correct answer, yet continuing to teach math to a room full of scientists. In order for him or her to become an expert at math, he or she would have to learn the formulas behind the problems.

No matter what your goal is, everything has to have a solid foundation in order to grow or withstand the elements. Be specific in what you want to become the expert at, study it, and learn all the variations around that one thing so that you fully understand the ins and outs. Practice doing it until it becomes effortless. Get the proper training if necessary, and teach it to see if there are gaps between theory and application. Make sure that whatever area you desire to become an expert in is something you are genuinely passionate about.

I consider myself a source of information, and I can assist people with the planning and mapping of goals, but unless they are active, nothing I give them will produce results. Do my clients believe I am an expert in the areas I assist them in? Yes. Why? Because they see the results of my efforts when it comes to the movements of their goals. I am teaching them from a place of three areas I make a point to excel in, in my personal path of establishing myself as an expert—experience, studied and applied knowledge, and personal results. The following story will give insight on how this can be applied in your life.

MOTHERHOOD

My friend Margo has a two-year-old son named Alexander. She awaited his arrival after being told she could not give birth for ten-plus years. "It's not going to happen, your eggs are not capable...," she was told. She was diligent in her own research and refused to give up. After many years of trying everything she could think of, she ended up with fertile eggs. She found a surrogate to carry for her, and there came one of the most amazing baby boys a family could ask for. Needless to say, she was protective of him, careful with him, in love with him. As Alexander got older, Margo had a hard time letting go of certain motherly duties such as carrying him everywhere, feeding him, cleaning up behind him, leaving him at pre-K, and treating him as if he was still only weeks old. How often do we hold on so tightly to relationships the same way regardless of how badly we are enabling the other person to grow?

Enabling is a nasty word that only hurts the one being enabled. One sibling doing everything for the other because they are younger, a co-worker covering for their friend whose late for work, or making excuses for your significant other's behavior instead of confronting him or her and being honest about what needs to change and why. Margo cried every time she dropped Alexander off at school, especially when he called for her as she walked away. She later found out that as soon as she was out of his sight, he'd run to play with the other kids, and was all of a sudden independent. When she would tell him to clean up his play area, it melted her heart to see his small frame bending down to pick up his own toys and put them away but he needed to learn responsibility. Sometimes we need to see the bigger picture and understand that hard decisions to sever accountability and responsibility are necessary in order to achieve growth and development. When Margo watched her son feed himself with the spoon turned completely side-ways, she wanted to take control and correct him or do it for him, but the right thing to do was let him practice on his own. Failure or not, until he got it for himself, he would not become an expert. Now he has learned the ins and outs of accomplishing a specific result for himself, and it will have his unique staple on it every time. Notice that Margo is also an expert. Her research proved a miracle in the eyes of doctors and she has created a business to educate and help other women with the same struggle to gain answers and solutions for fertility. Her expertise is priceless because she used her lack to fuel her drive and achieved well-executed results that go against the typical expected outcome. Sometimes people have to be left in a place where all they have is themselves to rely on to see what they are truly capable of. Enabling only frustrates the enabler and weakens the enabled, preventing that person from ever reaching his or her potential. This scenario is why it's imperative that we're passionate about what we want to become the expert at. I'm sure Margo's intentions were not to become an expert when she sought out the results she achieved; she simply wanted results and in turn became an expert. Nothing could stop her because in her mind; her baby being born was a must. For me, changing people's lives from the inside out through coaching and consulting is a must. What is *your* must? The one thing Margo and I have in common aside from our passion is that we both have to realize that <u>at some point</u> we have to let go. She as a mother, and myself as a coach. This is the only way the people we care about can be empowered to grow.

There will be times when you have to make the hard decision to sever the cord when dealing with or working with some people on one level or another. And even if you think they will hate you for it, if they have the capacity to understand this example and the power of what God is trying to produce from them, they will forgive you and do their best to achieve their goal(s) without you. Your path is your path and theirs is theirs. You may be that person who has been severed, and if you are, try your best to understand that the greatness inside you may never be fully birthed through the expectation that someone else will fill in the gaps for you. People are sometimes positioned in our lives to ignite the seeds within us, not to grow them into trees. An expert is only an expert by definition of what it produced. A farmer is an expert of the crops; the crops are experts of the fruit they bear. You may need to stand on your own to establish yourself as the expert. As long as there is someone there to carry you, how do you know what you are really capable of? Just like the mama bird nudges the baby bird from the nest, we must also be nudged so that we can soar. Come up with innovative ideas that propel your industry or passion in a new direction.

SHINE

Becoming an expert gives you credibility. Whether you produce hundreds of hours of podcasts or "how to" videos, make designer cakes that resemble any item people request, write a book, or have your own TV show, the consistency, legitimacy, and growth of information you provide will continue to establish you as an expert. Use what you have as a starting point and as long as you're moving toward what you want to accomplish in your actions, God will meet you there. The further you go, the further He will meet you. Do whatever you do with *excellence* and be open, learning more and growing as you go.

AFFIRMATIONS

I am an expert at _____.

I empower those around me to be great.

I shine in my lane.

Closing

If you feel that you struggle to shine, join the club! Lots of people constantly struggle, some shift in and out of the struggle, and others have mastered different areas of shining. My coaching practice, Coach Wright Consulting @kwrightcoaching.com is built on the very principles of this amazing acronym and helps people find their Purpose, Place, and Plan.

If you are seeking help with getting through the S.H.I.N.E.I.N.Y.O.U.R.L.A.N.E. process in your life, feel free to contact me to schedule one-on-one, group, or corporate coaching sessions.

Remember, just like directions on a plane when you are told to secure your oxygen mask first and then the child or person next to you, you can't help someone else and die in the process. There's a possibility that neither of you will make it. However, you have a better chance at helping them if you take the correct actions steps for yourself first.

I'm a firm believer that each person's trial is what helps another person journey through his or her own. If it weren't for others taking the time to write their stories, we wouldn't have access to some of the most powerful resources we need to overcome life's most challenging moments. At the right time, I ask that you write about your journey. Get your story out, even if it's just for you to refer back to when you need to ground yourself in humility to remember where you started. Someone needs to be encouraged every day, and you never know how your story may encourage someone or change his or her lifestyle for the better. The sooner we realize that we are here for others and not ourselves, the better off we will be. It's not about you and how you can make your life better; it's about the person hurting, in need, or on the verge of a breakdown and how making your life better can help them. The tone of this book is about focusing on yourself. That doesn't mean you can't observe others and take notes. But try to mimic what you see in them, seek what *you* have in an effort to be complete, and help someone else do the same.

Final Thought

The darkest hours are not that of the night but of the mind's inability to see the light... SHINE. -#CoachWright

ABOUT THE AUTHOR

Coach Kurinn Wright has dedicated her life to helping people see better, know better, do better, and live better. She is a native of Birmingham, AL. who spent several years in Southern California before settling in Atlanta GA. With thirteen plus years of experience in higher education, eight years of experience in life plan development, and a bachelor's degree in Human Resource Management, her expertise is in goal development, strategic planning, conducting focus groups, employee satisfaction, project management and career preparation. In addition, Coach Wright provides author coaching, and is co-owner of a business coaching company. Her practice is centered on the foundation of teaching people how to 'Shine In Their Lane' beginning with inner work that translates into action steps. In Coach Wright's past time, she writes fiction/mystery under a pen name and volunteers with youth organizations. To learn more about Coach Wright, or to acquire her services feel free to visit www.kwrightcoaching.com.

Manufactured by Amazon.com
Columbia, SC
10 April 2017